From
Couch to
Corporation

From Couch to Corporation

Becoming a Successful CORPORATE THERAPIST

Iris Martin

John Wiley & Sons, Inc.

New York • Chichester • Brisbane • Toronto • Singapore

Though this book is nonfiction, the names and distinguishing traits of all clients and individuals mentioned in the book have been changed.

This publication is designed to provide accurate and authoritative information in regard to the subject matter covered. It is sold with the understanding that the publisher is not engaged in rendering professional services. If legal, accounting, medical, psychological, or any other expert assistance is required, the services of a competent professional person should be sought.

Library of Congress Cataloging-in-Publication Data:

Martin, Iris, 1955–
    From couch to corporation : becoming a successful corporate
    therapist / by Iris Martin.
        p.   cm.
      Includes index.
      ISBN 0-471-11958-X (cloth : alk. paper)
    1. Psychology, Industrial.   2. Business consultants.
    3. Industrial psychologists.   4. Behavior therapists.   I. Title.
    HF5548.8.M3734   1996
    158.7—dc20   96-4890

Printed in the United States of America

10 9 8 7 6 5 4 3 2 1

For Ugaro and Nena, with love.

My husband, Robert Lessack, builder and artist, who cheerfully bears the burden of being my everything.

And for Seth and Josh, for accepting me.

FOREWORD

"It was the best of times, it was the worst of times." Charles Dickens' opening sentence to "A Tale of Two Cities" described Europe at the end of the Eighteenth Century, but it could be applied just as well to today's world, two centuries later. Indeed, for many professions, including that of psychologists, Dickens' sentence perfectly sums up the environment in which professionals are striving to make their living. Why should this be and in what ways can individuals take steps to eliminate or at least reduce the problems?

The reasons why the last decade of the twentieth century mirrors the last decade of the eighteenth century are many and can ultimately be summarized by the word "change." Change is neutral, being an agent either for good or for evil, but its impact on individuals is invariably disruptive. People by and large do not like change. Change is upsetting. It creates uncertainty and discomfort, removing the familiar and replacing it with the unknown, and yet change is good for individuals. Pejorative clichés, such as being "stuck in a rut," recognize the need for people to be forced to change. Indeed, one might argue that clinical psychologists and psychiatrists have built their profession on helping people come to terms with unexpected changing circumstances.

Like every other facet of human life, the individual demand for psychological and psychiatric services is changing. It may well be decreasing in society as a whole but a great opportunity is opening up for these professions in the wider field of commerce and industry.

Over the past century, corporate organizations have changed dramatically. Some of these changes reflect changes in society; others have themselves been agents for change in society.

A century ago, the American economy was dominated by the so-called "Robber Barons," individuals who wielded enormous power. Rockefeller's domination of the oil industry was mirrored in other industries by men such as J. P. Morgan, Carnegie, Vanderbilt, and Stanford. Over the next few decades, these men were succeeded by others such as Durant, Ford, Paterson, and Sloan, while Taylor started to comment and publish management texts on a more formal basis than hitherto. Gradually, the individual entrepreneur was superseded by the great corporations, and by the middle of the century, the economic scene was dominated by the great corporate entities. For the bulk of the working population, the impact of change was limited. They still were operating in an environment of command and control. The public environment in the 1950s, perhaps, was typified by *The Death of a Salesman* and *The Man in the Gray Flannel Suit*. Henry Ford's famous "Any color you want so long as it is black" had been replaced by IBM's dress code of white shirts and dark suits. The only change was the institutionalization of a paternal culture in which individuals still expected to have "jobs for life." In return for which they, as individuals, devoted their lives to the corporate goals. In such an environment, the employee who was prepared to subsume his (rarely her) individuality into the corporate culture had a comfortable and apparently secure life. Only those individuals who were, as the Japanese say, "nails which stuck up," were hammered down. Or, going back to Roman times and Tarquin the Proud, it was only the tall poppies whose heads were cut off. But the last quarter of this century has seen a dramatic change. For the individual, corporate downsizing and the associated employee layoffs has destroyed the concept of lifetime employment. At the same time, the shift from manufacturing towards service companies has led to other forms of disruptive change.

Perhaps the most significant of these changes, from the point of view both of the corporations themselves and their individual employees, is the need to focus on customers rather than on products. It is arguable that successful manufacturers always have focused on their customer needs. But, in practice, many manufacturers were able to focus solely on the product, either through quality or cost improvement. Their customer relationship was limited to meeting a limited number of customers' product specification. But companies in service industries usually have to deal with a plethora of individual customers whose needs are diverse and much less manageable by central control. Even McDonald's, perhaps the epitome of detailed specification, has had to expand its menu to meet customer requirements. Erstwhile public utilities, such as the telephone companies, have re-oriented themselves to provide better customer service, with a range of new services such as call-forwarding and voice mail. Whether all these new services are an improvement is not always apparent to users, but there undoubtedly has been a greater willingness to offer customers a wider range of services.

In banking and financial services, the changes perhaps have been as dramatic as in any industry. Old jokes such as the answer to the question "How do you approach your bank manager for a loan?" being "On your knees." are no longer true. Indeed, it is almost the reverse, with banks competing aggressively for any new business opportunities. The consequence of this change of economic emphasis from manufacturing to service companies has resulted in a need for change both among corporations and among their employees in the ways they organize and present themselves.

Greater diversity among customers' needs requires greater flexibility in dealing with these needs. This means that individuals dealing with those needs must have the power to meet them. But it is a contradiction to contemplate empowerment of individual employees with management structures that were inherited from an era of command and control. How can management reconcile this contradiction?

For the individual employee, the changes are equally wrenching. From an environment in which many employees could be satisfied that they had done their job once they had done everything which they had been given or asked to do, to an environment in which they are expected "to use their best judgment," is a major psychological shift. The pressures on the workers of production lines being speeded up are much more obvious than the pressures of asking white collars workers to "do their best." But the latter pressures, especially when coupled with downsizing, are certainly as great, albeit more insidious. So how can individuals learn to cope with these sorts of changes and pressures?

Both companies and their staff at all levels need help in adjusting to the new environment. Fortunately, such help is readily available. Unfortunately, some of the helpers are less able than others.

Traditionally, many consultants have specialized in the "hard" skills, many in a direct line of intellectual descent from Frederick Taylor and his "time-and-motion" skills. Equally, many other consultants have concentrated on the "softer" skills such as advising on strategy. But few have focused on the critical importance of ensuring that a company's culture changes to meet the changing world. And that means primarily changing the skills and, more important, the outlook of the people who work in that company. We all are familiar with companies whose slogan is a variation on the theme that the customer is king, but whose staff truly sees customers as an unwelcome disruption. Ensuring that intention and execution go together is extraordinarily difficult. It is in this area that Iris Martin and her psychotherapeutic consultants at CDM, Inc. have had a major contribution in helping management to change their identities, ideas, structures, objectives, training, and cultures.

Leading a company that is celebrating its Tercentenary, it is very obvious to me how much the world has changed since the Bank of Scotland's foundation in 1695. But how many times and in what ways has the Bank of Scotland had to change its business approach and philosophy? One does not know, but the importance of focus on enduring verities is apparent. A certain degree of flexibility or pragmatism obviously has helped. When in 1745, Bonnie Prince Charlie retreated from England to Edinburgh en route to his final defeat at Culloden, the Bank of Scotland's directors prudently retired with the Bank's bullion to the safety of Edinburgh Castle—and to make assurance double sure, lent the commander of the castle sufficient money to pay the garrison's wages! As Aesop's fable makes clear, the willow's flexibility can survive a gale which destroys an oak tree. Maintaining that flexibility is management's principal responsibility. And it is in this area that consultants like Iris Martin can contribute greatly. The Bank of Scotland has benefited from applying Iris's ideas and skills. We are grateful to her and to the CDM team. I hope that others can benefit. To paraphrase the British Chancellor's traditional ending to his Budget Speech: I commend this book to its readers.

PETER BURT
Chief Executive, Bank of Scotland

ACKNOWLEDGMENTS

Like my life, this book has been shaped by the people who have most inspired me. First, the many chief executives who have shared their lives and the inner world of their corporations have taught me firsthand that there is no true separation between the "self" of the leader and the organizational culture that he creates. There is a "collective unconscious" that permeates the environment of all organizations and regulates the upper limits on success and growth. In each client organization in which I've consulted, the company's upper limit can be traced back to an intrapsychic barrier within the CEO. As he (and it is still almost always "he") gains awareness and skill in his ability to transform aspects of himself, ceiling barriers to the organization's success disappear. Therefore, it becomes each corporate leader's responsibility to work on himself in order for growth and health to permeate his organization, no matter how deep and wide the self-examination journey may be. I've been privileged to guide that journey. Many times I have witnessed firsthand the subsequent impact that it has on improving corporate performance.

I've been extremely lucky in being in the right place at the right time both academically and professionally. When I was a psychology student in the 1970s in Philadelphia, family systems theory was the cutting edge focus of the clinical community. I was encouraged to incorporate this broader perspective into my emerging theoretical orientation. I was encouraged as well to be eclectic in developing an integrative psychotherapeutic style. This early exposure helped form my deepest belief that led to the CDM approach: Psychology as a technology has tremendous power in transforming the workplace; and clinicians can be invaluable resources to corporate executives.

Simultaneously, the management consulting industry where I gravitated following graduate school, was undergoing a similar revolution as well. Changing global business dynamics led the industry from being a unidimensional, operating solutions-based provider to becoming a partner to organizations seeking to catalyze change. Being a "shrink" of sorts, I was recruited to Gemini Consulting (United Research Company at that time), and encouraged to apply psychotherapeutic techniques. My role involved integrating clinical principles into traditional consulting processes with major corporations. These early experiments yielded positive, although unexpected results.

Brilliant, tenacious, experienced visionaries have taken both time and patience to imprint and champion me. The dynamics and power of these relationships, whether they have been with professors, bosses, therapists, or colleagues, have inspired me to create a consulting technology for the mentoring relationship as a vehicle for accelerating growth. When compared with the cognitive-analytic "left brain" approach, emotional learning through identification, transference, and introjection is a far more efficient learning process. Organizations needing to quickly indoctrinate and culturize their employees, can use mentoring to transmit values, styles, and strengths effectively. It is also the best strategy for keeping the vision and spirit of the organization alive as it undergoes the trials of transformation. Without my own mentors, I would lack the conviction to convince chief executives that not only does mentoring work, it is in fact, the "glue" that holds a transforming system together.

The following people are responsible for supporting this project:

- ○ My editor at John Wiley and Sons, Kelly Franklin, who has a love of psychology in addition to having the vision for this book, the tenacity to convince me to undertake it, and the patience required for birthing a new author.

- ○ My collaborator, Toni Reinhold, for her energy and discipline in translating my ideas, papers, and beliefs into a workable structure from which I could write.

- ○ My Corporate Therapy Seminar (CTS) psychotherapist graduates who critiqued every aspect of the *From Couch to Corporation* workshop that CDM provides for clinicians transisting into the corporate world. The CTS has been invaluable in further developing the application of the CDM model for psychotherapists.

- ○ Drs. Diana and Sam Kirschner, authors and psychotherapists currently in private practice, former co-directors of the

Institute for Comprehensive Family Therapy (CFT), and mentoring supervisors to CDM's consultant staff. The results achieved at their center, with therapy cases managed by themselves and their faculty, were the early inspiration for me to build a psycho-operational consulting model for corporations undergoing transformation. In watching the Kirschners teach and work together, as well as with us, I was convinced that their innovative approach to family and individual treatment, which incorporates the progressive abreactive regressive model (PAR) for transformation within the context of a reparenting therapeutic relationship (conceived by Dr. Arthur Stein in 1980), had profound implications for corporate life. Without the Kirschner's direct involvement, CDM would have not been able to apply their model to the business world. Without their mentoring, I would not have been able to convince CEOs of the value of such a powerful intervention. For everything they have given to their students, clients, and supervisees over the decade during which I've been associated with them, I speak for many when I say that we are extremely grateful and positively impacted.

o David Teiger, former Chairman and CEO of United Research Company and then of Gemini Consulting, had the original vision to integrate aspects of clinical psychology into management consulting processes. It was David who first encouraged CEOs to utilize psychology as a technology. Over the last decade, David as my mentor, was the source of energy and inspiration for the creation and success of Creative Dimensions in Management, Inc. Our relationship served as the conceptual model for CDM's mentoring approach. As the builder of United Research and Gemini Consulting, David is affectionately held up by clients and staff alike as the embodiment of what a business leader should be. His vision remains our inspiration, and so many of us carry him inside of us.

o Jennifer Buton Tallow has been actively involved in translating our approach into pragmatic business applications since 1986. Her contribution in the last decade is deeply appreciated. In addition to being a trustworthy and valued colleague, she has been a great friend and global traveling companion.

- Jack Gitterman, M.D., my link to the world of psychiatry, has been a role model of what a psychotherapist should be. His forty years as a practitioner and supervisor illustrated weekly why he always knew the right thing to do next, in response to a variety of therapeutic dilemmas and opportunities.

- Peter Kuriloff, Ph.D., encouraged my graduate research studies at the University of Pennsylvania in 1978–1980, and became my conscience for later writing endeavors, and my internalized advocate for clinical supervision.

- John Gordon, Ph.D., currently in practice as an innovative neuropsychologist, gave me my first exposure to psychology at Temple University. Through his eyes, psychology captivated and dazzled me. Without John, I would not have had the courage to relentlessly pursue psychotherapeutic interventions within the corporation.

- Suzy Wales helped start the CDM London office in 1987 and build our staff and reputation in the United Kingdom. Suzy also "anglicized" our approach and rallied the British psychotherapeutic community around our work. Also thanks to Mike Kaplin, Clive Ley, Mike Milan, Mike Turner, Christine Fitzpatrick, and Sol Davison for excellent work in the UK practice.

- The Lafferty Organization and IBM, for introducing and promoting our consulting approach internationally.

- Peter Emanuelle, the spiritual source for CDM consulting products, including the culture transformation process, mentoring, and most recently, AGLS (Accelerated Growth Learning System). It is my privilege to be a vehicle for his ideas and wisdom.

- Jack Lin for demonstrating the true meaning of commitment in relationship to me.

- The Sisterhood: Georgette Baginsky, Ingrid Graeff, Marji Altman Bershad, Lesa Edelman, Fran Warkow, Bethie Lin, Vickie Smith, Becky Lessack, Cindy Levinson, Sandy Radich, and Penny Olstein. My girlfriends are my greatest blessing in life.

- Maria Chellis, best-selling author and close friend, convinced me that I could be an author. Her brilliance, generous spirit, and unconditional support always astounded me.

- Ranee Gumm, Ph.D., for the vision to apply AGLS technology to accelerating the achievement of operational improvement.

- David Mulvey, Vicky Carruthers, AJ and Scooter, Joe McGoneagle, the late Robert Monroe, and the staff of the Monroe Institute for allowing CDM the use of their facilities for our staff trainings. For us, HemiSync is a reliable freeway to accelerating self-growth.

- Pat Smith and Joan McFadden for the preparation of the final document and their dedication to its completion.

- The CDM psychotherapist consultants, for keeping the work alive, evolving, prospering, and on the cutting edge of the international management consulting industry.

IRIS MARTIN

CONTENTS

PART THREE

Doing Corporate Therapy

PART FOUR

Your Competitive Advantage in Corporate Therapy

PART ONE

Psychology and the Workplace

1

Psychology in the Corporation: Why Now?

The boom and bust years of the 1980s were more than just a classic swing of the global economic pendulum. The shift from easily earned megabucks to lean and hard times triggered radical changes in the way corporations around the world do business.

In the United States, the dramatic and swift change from rapid economic growth to reduced bottom lines permanently changed the face of corporate America. It also impacted the way Americans would define their future role within the workplace.

When the United States slipped into recession in the early part of the 1990s, Americans expected cutbacks and layoffs. Unlike past recessions, however, the recession of the early 1990s introduced a radical rethinking of the structure, size, and composition of the corporation. Organizations took more than just a critical look at their staff sizes and how they could save money. With the emergence of information technology coupled with process reengineering, the capability for dramatic, permanent headcount reduction was real.

Anticipated layoffs through attrition evolved into radical downsizing. For the first time, these affected not only the blue collar, but the white collar ranks, and reached the sacrosanct upper echelon of management. More Americans were declared jobless than had been out of work during the Great Depression. Many economists argued that the United States had lapsed into a depression; not a recession. The manufacturing sector led this descent, but no part of the economy was left undisturbed.

3

Downsizing was so severe and widespread, that many people caught in the crunch found themselves unable to readily move from one employer to another. Thousands of Americans found themselves literally without careers as entire departments were suddenly eliminated. Confronting the prospect of having to re-educate themselves in completely different lines of work regardless of their age, tenure, and life stage, their reactions ranged from panic to rage.

Homes and other trappings of success were often lost. Young people who had made quick fortunes on Wall Street were deeply in debt from living beyond their means. Middle-aged men and women who had been comfortably entrenched in senior management positions found themselves without their high-paying jobs and benefits. There were often not comparable positions in other industries.

As corporate America restructured, retooled, and permanently cut costs and staff sizes, many organizations merged to inherit new markets. Consequently, corporations undertook a radical rethinking of their mission and direction. The word "vision" was born to corporate America. Employees were asked to adopt an organization's "vision" for its future or risk being left behind. As it undertook dramatic, painful change programs to fulfill its vision, the lean, mean, newly focused corporation created a culture that embodied its new values and goals.

Those willing to work toward the vision quickly discovered that this meant learning a new trade, or multiple trades, so that reduced staffs could do the work once done by teams. Supporting the vision also meant a major shift in identity, style, and role. No one was safe to "stay in the box." As the context of the corporation shifted to become more competitive, responsive, and cost-effective, people were forced to transform themselves as well in order to survive.

Corporate America was not prepared for the depth of change brought about by the economic downturn of the early 1990s. Traditional business models proved to be ineffective tools, as systemic, rather than historical and functional solutions were needed. Past performance could not be relied upon to predict and forecast the future, as the impact of such total transformation was not yet known. Bottom-line improvement, once targeted at an annual growth of 15 percent, shot up to projections of 25 percent or higher. The pressure felt by management and employees became enormous.

The financial impact of such unpredictable change was illustrated by the high number of failed mergers. The tasks of integrating two entirely different cultures proved more complex than it appeared. Clearly there were psychological dynamics to manage that required a conscious strategic approach.

The psychological impact of such change also paralyzed the internal culture. Corporations found their employee populations stuck, unable to address the many new challenges. Attempts at culture transformation were fragmented knee-jerk reactions. Often, the interlocking systemic effects were not understood. As a result, many initial attempts at culture change were poorly designed and subsequently failed.

Since the industrial revolution, corporations have recognized the need to go outside their own organizations for assistance. Particularly in the past four decades, many have turned with increasing frequency to management consultants for help. In response, virtually all of the major international management consultancies have now created a "change management" division. These groups provide process interventions and support services for organizations undergoing change.

Their consulting staffs, however, are neither trained nor experienced to deliver complex psychological interventions. Because of this lack of psychological training, many traditional management consultants do not appreciate the impact on corporate and individual psyches that is created by intense rapid change.

Yet, the root cause of most problems that plague the corporation is often hidden in its collective psyche. Not having the tools nor training to correctly diagnose the psyche/system dynamic, these consultants are unable to offer effective long-lasting solutions. Therefore, interventions are short-term and often fail. Particularly, the quality improvement programs delivered by consultants during the 1980s were disappointing in their ability to provide long-term ongoing benefits. Other consulting trends have damaged the industry's long-term credibility as well.

Conversely, psychotherapists are supremely suited for supporting organizational change. Trained in group processes as well as individual analysis; sensitive to developmental milestones and transitions; educated in the formation of beliefs, perceptions, and behavior patterns; the clinician brings a dazzling tool kit to the corporation's dilemmas. Able to see the relationship between history, people and process, and skilled in both direct and indirect strategic interventions; the therapist excels in bringing about rapid change expertly and subtly. Corporate clients often view clinicians more as magicians than consultants, impressed by their depth and perceptivity.

Until recently, the exposure of psychologists and psychiatrists to the corporate world has been limited to the private clients that they treat. Yet, the extent of their exposure was destined to change along with the corporate environment. As organizations faced radical transformation, the world of psychotherapy was similarly being shaken by external forces. Profitable psychotherapeutic interventions with children, adults, and families were rapidly diminishing. Changes in insurance healthcare programs and reimbursement policies reduced the duration of psychotherapy. The advent of health care reforms further impacted client load. Even psychotherapists with long term, robust private practices now see a steady decline in referrals and appointments.

The tragedy in this is while the complexity of change demands more psychological growth now than ever before, less support is currently available. With channels for third party payment drying up and private patients' economic security threatened, the psychotherapeutic industry is thus forced to consider creative delivery channels. Currently, the corporation is fertile ground for psychotherapists with an entrepreneurial spirit.

The demand for personal and professional growth in corporate America is steadily increasing. The need for a comprehensive strategic approach to managing change is evident as well. As current attempts at accelerating change have been of limited effectiveness, a new opportunity for applied psychology has been created. And the need for it has never been greater than it is today.

As psychotherapists examine their bottomlines, many are shifting to the corporate arena. Those transisting from couch to corporation may seem daunted by the language, culture and context of business at first. However, many of the tools used in organizational consulting are similar to those used in private practice. While the focus of corporate therapy is on performance improvement rather than symptom alleviation, the interventions often have a clinical origin. Straddling the clinical and business domains is possible and can become quite comfortable with experience. Yet the transition is harrowing and requires guidance and support.

The purpose of this book is to provide a blueprint to assist the psychotherapist who is moving from a clinically-based private practice into providing psychotherapeutic consulting services to organizations.

The timing is exquisite. The business world is in as much dire need for psychological intelligence as the private practitioner is in need of clients who can afford to pay. Healthcare reform has created enough thunder (the devaluing of psychological services by insurance providers) and lightning (the burst of insight that other markets for psychotherapeutic services exist) to send a wave of clinicians into the management consulting industry; repositioning their credentials and repackaging their skills.

Yet, this transition is not merely a career change. As employer of clinicians for over a decade, I have witnessed firsthand the profound transformation that they face when attempting to practice within the corporate context. Changes in role, identity, image, capability and focus are only a few of the rites of passage inherent in this complex transition. And the ones who begin the journey often doubt that success is even possible. Talented clinicians tell me they fear leaving the safe confines of their office to encounter the confusing maze of divisions and departments which is the typical corporation.

Many challenges must be successfully overcome as part of the rite of passage from private to corporate practice. They include:

- ○ Creating a consulting service and product line that meets the needs of the targeted corporate market while platforming and showcasing various clinical talents, specialties and successes.

- ○ Learning the inner workings of the business world as well as various industry technologies in order to establish the credibility needed to secure consulting contracts.

- ○ Adapting to the new language and rituals of the business world while simultaneously observing and dispelling its myths and illusions.

- ○ Marketing oneself through the use of business cards, brochures, presentations and seminars.

- ○ Protecting oneself legally and financially in a new career with different boundaries, ethical implications and professional liabilities then a clinical practice.

- ○ Establishing contacts within corporations that lead to meeting with qualified decision makers who control management services budgets and authorize consultancy projects.

- Mastering a sales process which includes approaching the decision-maker, undertaking a needs analysis, designing a project proposal, closing the contract, and measuring results.

- Building a consulting practice distinguished from the competition based on a timeless positioning that can be communicated through a simple tag line.

These are only some of the practical tasks that the clinician must master. There are intrapsychic and interpersonal challenges as well:

- Coping with fantasies of failure that surface with a monumental change in career identity. These manifest somatically (the nausea accompanying the first sales call) or reside as inner voices discouraging one from making any possible contribution to the business world at all.

- The initial terror of having to physically go onsite for a client visit. It's one thing to think about leaving one's office to do this new kind of work. An altogether different barrier exists when visiting a prospective client to make the pitch.

- Managing the grief of losing the "doctor knows best" image when consulting in a corporate environment; where "Ph.D." often means "mindreader" and the less said about a clinical background, the better.

- Proactively competing for business against aggressive management consultants who want to control the lion's share of the corporate consulting budget.

- Preparing the family for your entrance into the corporate world. This will include subscriptions to publications such as *Industry Week, Forbes, Fortune,* and *The Wall Street Journal* and an obsession with the daily activities of the world's financial markets. This often entails a change in your image as well: trading in tweed blazers for Armani suits and Italian loafers.

- Being comfortable as an advisor to corporate clients, who are often amazed by the psychotherapist's ability to apply clinical principles to business operations and then devise viable solutions that work. (Executives are truly impressed by the lightening quick ability clinicians have in applying complex psychological concepts to a variety of everyday business problems).

While your transformation to "corporate therapist" may be overwhelming, it is not without substantial rewards. You will be highly prized by your corporate clients. Although developmentally and characterologically similar to many of your clinical cases, they are more highly functioning and therefore extremely grateful for clinical expertise and support. They give back exponentially as well, through providing introductions and referrals.

While it is expected that you will feel a sense of trepidation, even doom, in embarking on this new career, look at what you have already accomplished! You have received advanced degrees and a license to practice psychology. You have succeeded in a clinical setting or an entrepreneurial private practice. Having come this far in your professional life, your transition into the business world is a logical next step.

Remember that a highly trained, conceptual, academic mind generally finds business principles easy to grasp. Therefore, your finely honed ability to observe, listen, and analyze on simultaneous levels will flourish within the corporate setting. As a result, your recommendations will be comprehensive and multidimensional. This will give you a competitive advantage over most traditional management consultants. They may understand business better, but they are not trained in interpreting dynamics or predicting behavior.

The corporate market has never been more receptive for psychological expertise and support. In fact, the need for psychotherapeutic intervention will become insatiable as we move into the twenty-first century, as even a greater pace of change will be needed. For those contemplating a corporate therapy practice, the time to train is now.

2

You, Too, Can Be a Corporate Therapist

My own career as a corporate therapist was founded in tragedy. Upon leaving a project site some sixteen years ago, I discovered a dead sparrow smashed and smeared across the windshield of my rental car. At that time, I was a fledgling staff-level consultant on assignment to a Fortune 500 client. Desperately wanting to be home before midnight on a Friday night, I found myself impeded by the carcass trapped by my windshield wipers. Clinically astute, I felt sympathy for the plight of the stiff drenched bird, who fatally miscalculated the height of the car. Unfamiliar with the dignified, discreet disposal of dead animals, I set off for a broom, washcloth and hopefully, janitorial assistance as backup. I stumbled instead into the middle-aged paunch of the chief executive; keys in hand, also longing to head home. The night was grim. There was a dismal dark downpour that kept images of Truman Capote's *In Cold Blood* unfolding in my mind.

Initially, it was our equal desperation and sex-role programming that bonded the CEO and me. Observing his tee shirt and khakis, I assumed that he was the plant custodian. He thought that I was a transient damsel in distress. Once positioned, we acted out our internalized gender scripts efficiently. Eager to dispose of the job at hand, he gallantly offered to remove the bird and send it humanely into the hereafter. I agreed to Windex the windshield and headlights to remove its more scattered remains. By the end of this grisly ordeal, we were friends. We had altruistically sacrificed our narcissistic needs for food, warmth, and marital harmony at the most critical juncture of the weekend: Friday night. Instead, we had dedicated ourselves to providing the unknown sparrow with a karmically correct passing on.

This experience created a certain bond between us. It followed that the CEO would then invite me back to his executive suite to phone my husband while he phoned his wife. Both of us separately explained why any hope of romance for that evening had literally been washed away. My husband was magnanimous and supportive of my attempt at androgyny. The CEO's wife was less spiritually predisposed. She demanded that he travel immediately to a local restaurant to make a prescheduled corporate appearance. He rolled his eyes and acquiesced, then abruptly took her off the speakerphone.

This event was the first in a series of privileged glimpses into the existential dilemma of the CEO. While I was clearly susceptible to the mystique of corporate life propagandized by the media, instead I kept slamming up against reality. The CEO was a regular guy[1] generally caught up in a world of trouble. Under tremendous pressure from unrealistic expectations, he was expected to remain focused, objective, selfless, and in control. Existentially, the job that he had sought over a career of personal sacrifices led to both depression and enticement. Clearly, he needed a shrink. Once created, my role evolved into a combination business strategist and family therapist. Out of these initial interactions later evolved the CDM credo: transform the CEO; transform the organization. The work always starts at the top.

But at that time, based upon tradition and industry standards, I was technically prohibited from interacting with chief executives. In my twenties, I had not yet passed the various rites of passage within the firm that employed me. So this bird incident was both fortuitous and risky. It led to an instant, albeit unusual rapport between the CEO and me as well as a severe reprimanding by my superiors. However, this particular CEO facilitated my extrication by seeking my counsel aggressively. So there I was, doing what I did best, without much of a name for it. It did however, lead to increased billing and therefore was begrudgingly allowed. And since there was no prescribed role, there were few defined boundaries. I consulted on matters of business, family, psyche, and spirit. Later, the term "mentor" seemed appropriate and innocuous enough to clients and colleagues alike.

---

[1] The masculine gender is used throughout the book for simplicity, recognizing that the individuals could be either male or female.

I was getting quite an education from this lofty perspective. Encouraged to read business plans, operating reports, machine maintenance manuals and management textbooks, I felt compelled to learn the manufacturing and marketing processes of my client's organizations as well. This often included making a sample product myself, by following an operator's step-by-step instructions; or accompanying salesmen to listen to customers ideas, needs, and complaints firsthand.

I also witnessed the agonies associated with being a senior executive. Many of my clients were forced to fire long-standing colleagues to meet unexpected budget cuts. Others experienced humiliation from losing millions on a poorly implemented plan. The media's often inaccurate analyses of the causes of bad quarterly earnings horrified many CEOs as well.

The new world of business intoxicated me and in those early years, everyone was my teacher. The hourly workers, intimately knowledgeable about making products showed me the complexities of manufacturing. The maintenance workers, surgeons of huge pieces of equipment that could make or lose millions, taught me the need for disciplined reporting. The front-line supervisors, who had to ensure output without killing creativity, demonstrated the need for interpersonal skills. The middle managers, who saw profit-making opportunities but had little power in funding them, illustrated the need for empowerment. And the chief executives, who having gotten the job, immediately wondered who on earth would want it, validated the need for corporate therapy. I felt quite grateful for observing this new world firsthand with the benefit of a clinically trained eye.

As I experimented with utilizing clinical strategies and techniques in my consulting practice, I found business results were forthcoming faster. Also, morale steadily improved. For example, respecting confidentiality I found was the exception rather than the rule within the management consulting industry. Many clients told me of betrayals by consultants who reported confidences back to bosses. My psychotherapeutic training had made me more sensitized to the vulnerability that corporate clients feel when opening their organization to outsiders.

Further, there were countless opportunities in which clinical theory could be applied. I found that object relations, developmental psychology, neurolinguistic programming, neuropsychology and family systems theory as well as others yielded direct benefit in providing both short-and long-term solutions. Granted, the context and dynamics of corporate therapy were different than private practice. But when carefully managed, results could be greater. For example, I discovered empirically that the "collective unconscious" within the corporation transmitted learning systemically. What people learned in their workplace was quickly taken home for use with their families.

I had found an unexpected home for my academic training and psychological expertise and to my surprise, I found my business clients as eager to learn clinical models as I was to name the individual parts of a plastic injection molder.

Once installed in my corporate therapy career, I also experienced a meteoric rise in popularity among the client's people. I progressed from the perception that "I think that Iris was brought in to make curtains for the machines" to "Iris can help get your ideas heard while still keeping her mouth shut." This phenomenon did not go unnoticed by the management consulting industry at large. I was soon receiving job offers from prestigious consultancies to "do something psychological" for their Fortune 500 clients.

I accepted an offer from United Research Company (URC) in 1981, a blue chip consultancy to the Fortune 500 (now Gemini Consulting). I felt that URC was capable of providing me with training and support in integrating psychotherapeutic principles and techniques into a broad range of consulting processes. I was quickly assigned to a small team of consultants reporting directly to the firm's Chief Executive and Chairman, David Teiger. Always the visionary, David predicted that psychology could be a technology important to CEOs, facing an ever-increasing pace of change to be managed. At the urging of URC's CEO clients, David had created a "blueprint" for CEOs, outlining strategic steps to follow in implementing major change. The "CEO Blueprint" translated clinically, was a systemic intervention designed to bring about business transformation. David encouraged me to experiment with the CEO Blueprint through pilot implementations with sophisticated CEO clients of Fortune 100 organizations.

Several years of constant travel later, my first husband demanded that I choose between married life and management consulting. Weeping in David's office at the thought of giving up my beloved career, he encouraged me to "be my biggest competitor." Armed with the CEO Blueprint that he generously bequeathed to me, I founded Creative Dimensions in Management, Inc. (CDM). My vision for it was to be a support services firm solely devoted to chief executives engineering a transformation of their organization. Since its conception in 1985, CDM has grown to be an international consultancy with multimillion dollar annual billings. Although we have attracted a highly prestigious global client list; we are not even close to being Gemini's biggest competitor. And yet, I wonder that without David as a mentor, I might still be a staff consultant, once disciplined by an exasperated plant superintendent during a plant tour. "Honey, if you move one inch closer to that lathe, that blade is liable to suck you in and snap your neck off." he said sharply. "You sure know nothin' around here."

CDM has created practical technologies for chief executives determined to effect a culture transformation, defined as a fundamental mindset change leading to transformed business performance. The CDM approach has evolved into a simultaneous focus on the leadership potential of management; through a corporate-wide individual and group mentoring program; the customer relationship; through a psychological analysis, sales process redesign, new subsequent product or service offerings; and a restructuring of operational processes that drive the business. We offer stand alone culture transformation programs, as well as partner with other consultancies who specialize in various aspects of organizational change.

In the last decade, CDM has worked with many Fortune 500 Chief Executives. We also assist fast-growing regional market leaders. CDM's staff are primarily psychotherapists who have made a transition from community service or private practice into full or part-time CDM project work. Consulting assignments last from three weeks to three years and are both domestic and foreign-based.

Throughout this odyssey, I have personally had the privilege of working intimately with chief executives and their significant others, including investment bankers, merger and acquisition firms, advertising and public relations agencies, and information technology suppliers. Together, we have formed multidisciplinary teams aligned to deliver the business vision.

My role, unlike others, however, has had the advantage of having fluid and permeable boundaries. This has allowed me to contribute to initiatives in which CDM played only an advisory role. Typical projects have included restructuring Boards, recruiting new senior management teams, selecting an advertising agency, approaching and acquiring a suitable merger partner, creating new products and services, and dissecting and downsizing obsolescent bureaucracies. In addition to directing the implementation of large CDM culture transformation projects, I am a psychotherapist and mentor to the CEO client and his family during the consulting engagement.

Some of CDM's successes have been to integrate merging cultures; to improve the cross-selling of financial products into the global banking world; to teach reluctant technical professionals the process of relationship selling; and to increase product sales through transforming their perceived value. We also create a healthy, growth-oriented culture among impassioned members of family businesses, who have gotten lost within their complex dynamics. When the unconditional love expected in families gets confounded by the conditional love inherent in corporations, both their current and future survivals are at stake.

In our practice, we have received invaluable clinical supervision from many of the profession's most brilliant and accomplished family therapists, psychoanalysts, group process experts, and neuropsychologists. In attempting to break up the homeostasis of the organization, the corporate therapist can quickly become engulfed and misled. Supervision has been the backbone of CDM projects; from weekly support of each team member, to four weeks of offsite clinical training per year.

Within my own client case load, I found that my personal and professional barriers required relentless confrontation. As a result, I won't work without clinical supervision. The magnitude and complexity of combined systemic and individual work opens up simultaneous change on the structural, strategic, operational, inter-and intradepartmental, interpersonal, intrapsychic, even spiritual fronts. Without a roadmap and a highly experienced clinical supervisor, one can quickly be consumed in the client organization's negative transference.

Having now heard my story, you know that you too can be a CEO therapist, or a corporate therapist at any level of an organization, for that matter. In fact, the breadth and depth of your clinical training and experience will make you a highly sought after advisor. For example, after a board meeting, I ran into a vice president who was being mentored by a CDM staff psychotherapist. Upon asking him how his mentoring was going, he quickly replied, "Well, you know, Iris, Mike is great. Not only does he keep me from projecting onto the team and denying the reality of bad performance, he points out when my repetition compulsion is rearing its ugly head; and how I then try to sabotage myself. My boss has been attempting a role reversal with me, and if I don't watch out, he can seduce me into my parentified child stuff. Oh, he also helped write my speech for Tokyo next week using NLP techniques. Tonight, we'll rehearse it at home with the wife and kids."

As this typical comment illustrates, you will find the corporate community mystified and fascinated by your clinical knowledge. Your business clients will eagerly internalize your teachings, language, psychological concepts, and models. They will often then surprise you by applying psychology to life circumstances with positive and gratifying results.

Consider the skills and talents that you already have as a psychotherapist that will support your couch to corporation transition:

1. *You are an expert at forming and building a trusting relationship.* The most significant element of the consulting process is the client relationship. Skills that you take for granted, like bonding, empathizing, confronting and disciplining, are a competitive advantage in the consulting industry.

2. *You have multidimensional training and experience.* Organizational life is complex; and you will find your deeper analysis of the issues useful. The corporate client may not see a problem as intrapsychic, as well as interpersonal, structural or systemic. As a result, he will appreciate your broader perspective.

3. *You are hypervigilant and tuned in to people.* This makes you keenly aware of the symbolic aspects of what you observe. Clients, particularly when recruiting executives, find this ability extraordinary in preventing bad hiring decisions that literally cost millions.

4. *You have conducted psychotherapy with extremely challenging cases, including borderlines and multiple personalities.* As such, you have experienced firsthand the commitment required for healing. Your ability to stay in close proximity with organizations undergoing the turbulence and pain of change will reap rewards from your grateful clients. Particularly artful transformation of negative transference is admired.

Take a deep breath and journey with me from couch to corporation! Enclosed are tools that you will need. In a year from now it will seem quite ordinary to take the elevator up to the executive suite, and eagerly get to work.

3

The World of the Corporation and the Role of the Corporate Therapist

Before undertaking a major transformation of your psychotherapeutic career, it is crucial that you realistically appraise the corporate arena. Just as certain realities apply to the therapeutic context, there are realities inherent in the corporate world. Some of these have created the perfect context for corporate therapy to thrive. Some of my own learnings illustrate that the timing is correct for your couch to corporation transition.

EVERY CHIEF EXECUTIVE OFFICER NEEDS A CORPORATE THERAPIST

The myriad responsibilities of the chief executive are becoming increasingly paradoxical. Consequently, the experience of executive leadership is becoming schizophrenic (see Figure 3.1). The CEO is expected to be a lover of people while being a slasher of headcount. He must be a creative visionary as well as a predator; ready to pounce on less fit organizational prey. He is a seducer of the masses as well as a schemer for profits. Who can play such diverse roles without becoming confused by their contradictory nature? Chief executives require psychological training to help them see that splits in the self are not only

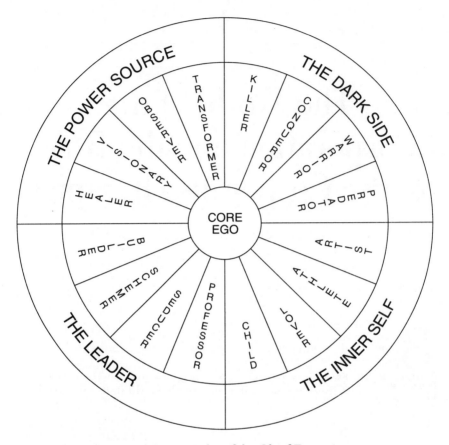

Figure 3.1   The Contradictory Roles of the Chief Executive.

associative but necessary for leadership. A crucial function of the corporate therapist can be to help the CEO manage the inherent complexity of his role.

I have found that once the hallowed halls of the chief executive's suite have become familiar to the well-intentioned corporate therapist, most CEOs are quite receptive to psychological input. They recognize that their personal growth has dramatic impact on their leadership skills, as well as on the development and success of their organizations.

But not all CEOs are hungry for self awareness. It takes only a glimpse into this month's business publications to witness the impact of chief executives masochistically inclined and otherwise, who are naive enough to believe in the omnipotent "Father-Knows-Best" illusion. However, these days it takes only one well-promoted s̲c̲.̲.̲.̲ to sufficiently humble them. As they review decisions that led to their demise, they often accept their own vulnerability. Armed with this insight, they become more receptive to self examination.

Many CEOs have had some experience with psychotherapy as a result of divorce, remarriage, career problems or their own recovery from an addiction or physical illness. Their experience has often impressed them with the power of psychology. They have often remarked that it is unfortunate that this sophisticated knowledge of people, growth and dynamics is not available to them in the workplace. Correctly, they recognize that executives who have influence over people would benefit from deeper self awareness and that psychology needs a larger domain.

Chief executives are typically surrounded by board members, business associates and weekend sports buddies, who when unqualified to be of clinical assistance, often recommend a psychotherapist. Some have gone as far as to arrange for one to strategically appear on the scene.

I began one of my most challenging consulting projects after I was confidentially contacted by a CEO's secretary. She watched me on a television talk show and thought that her boss and I should work together. As the keeper of his diary, she juggled his schedule to make time for our first meeting, as well as creatively facilitated our introduction. She did not worry that he would be offended by her taking it upon herself to "bring in a shrink." As a trusted insider, she knew that he respected her judgment.

ARE CEOs SUPERHEROES?

It is important for the corporate therapist to acknowledge his or her own internalized image of the chief or senior executive if only as a countertransferential issue. In Chapter 8, I'll discuss marketing strategies and how to attract clients and find your way in the corporate world. But at this juncture, you should have a realistic picture of who CEOs and senior executives really are.

Executives are romanticized in motion pictures, television dramas, and published profiles as superheroes. In reality, they are extremely high achievers who are burdened by daily unrealistic demands. A corporate therapist can be the low key yet invaluable resource to an executive as he grapples with the desire to accomplish as much as possible in a role that offers little job security or tenure. He often needs psychological input in considering his options.

The existential dilemma of the chief executive is complex and ironic. He has obvious authority, but is often powerless to change the people who implement his vision. He gets support from his board, but can't risk appearing conflicted. He values his family, but doesn't see them enough. He has friends, but they often have a hidden agenda. Can he be called upon for raising money or future employment?

The psychological leap from senior executive to chief executive is unexpected and enormous. With it comes an entirely new identity in which, quite literally, "the buck stops here." It requires the loss of a team of colleagues; many of whom the CEO has "grown up" with in the organization. As contenders and competitors for his new job, the fledging CEO recognizes the illusionary nature of intimacy with him now. As anxieties mount, the newly appointed CEO can unconsciously lure a direct report into an inappropriate role reversal. In this dead end dance, the subordinate is entrusted with the CEO's thoughts. He is then scapegoated, when unable to adequately address the CEO's concerns.

Most senior executives aspire to the CEO's chair, fantasizing that they alone hold the key to the organization's competitive advantage. Yet once installed in the executive suite, the implications of this new role are overwhelming. A corporate therapist can be the guide who leads the newly appointed CEO toward building an identity and business vision. The corporate therapist can also help him to leave his legacy. When the CEO retires, a new vision, post corporate life, can then be constructed in which new dreams can be fulfilled.

As the person who reports directly to the chief executive, many executives find themselves in a race against time. With only five or ten years left in a career that has spanned three decades, there is urgency to make one's mark. Rather than acknowledging that the top tier of management is of itself a noble accomplishment, many senior executives are frustrated CEOs. While appearing to support the chief, they foster hidden agendas and covertly thwart the vision. With political savvy, they often create multiple realities within the culture. This in turn confuses their subordinates as to the direction and priorities of the senior executive team.

The corporate therapist can be helpful in assisting the senior executive accept the limits of his role. As part of his own self-transformation journey, the senior executive can find new channels for creati   , can realize that being a CEO isn't all it appears to be.

PSYCHOLOGY AS A MAINSTREAM TECHNOLOGY

I would be hardpressed to find someone who is unfamiliar with the self-help movement, as it is promoted daily on every talk show on television. The extensive and intense marketing of self growth is partly responsible for psychotherapy leapfrogging its way into the collective consciousness of mainstream America.

Psychotherapy has evolved from being reserved for "crazy" people to becoming an acceptable support system for all people seeking personal growth. We now recognize that everyone encounters growth barriers; including the Princess of Wales and several U.S. Presidents.[1] The prime time broadcasting of the trauma and tragedy associated with growth is now an exercise in collective cleansing and healing. Both the "victims" interviewed on television and the at-home viewers mutually acknowledge this difficult struggle for selfhood.

The net result of participative talk show psychotherapy is an ever-increasing comfort level with self-disclosure. It is now okay, even admirable, to reveal one's problems to the American public. While increasing one's own popularity, the overall benefit of such disclosures has been to give permission for viewers to seek healing as well.

When I started my corporate therapy career in 1980, the acceptance of psychotherapy as a viable solution for everyday business problems was unheard of. Labels such as "child abuser," "alcoholic," and "borderline," were not typically used in polite conversation, let alone in the company cafeteria. There was little human resource assistance for employees with personal problems. The notion that the chief executive himself might be from a dysfunctional family could almost be cause for dismissal.

Now, the attitudinal shift toward psychotherapy in society as well as in the corporation is staggering. The following example from my own corporate therapy practice is an illustration. At an annual meeting, the chief executive, in full view of his management team and several thousand employees, unexpectedly called me onto the dais. He

---

[1] T. Reeves, A *Question of Character: Exploding the Kennedy Myth*. (New York: Random House, 1991).

then presented me with a corporate pin, claiming that I have helped him "unload the baggage of the past." His words were met by tears and cheers from his employees and family members. Far from being stereotyped as a "cry baby," this move was viewed by the organization as implicit permission to heal themselves. At the reception that followed, an outpouring of the personal tragedies experienced by his employees was directed toward my CDM team and me. Shortly thereafter, we expanded our mentoring program.

THE CORPORATE FAMILY IS SHRINKING

In the past, employees found comfort in their "family" of colleagues within the workplace. Having one family at home and another one at work kept many employees bonded to one organization for much of their working lives. Today, however, that family is gone due to mergers, restructuring, and downsizing. The dissolution of the corporate family coincided with the breakdown of the at-home family through increased divorces. Two sources relied upon for support suddenly disappeared.

The impact of this on performance is significant. Organizational changes, once processed through intimate contact with trusted significant others, are dealt with silently now. Self-destructive behaviors such as alcohol abuse or over-eating have increased, leading most corporations to establish employee assistance programs. Trusted corporate elders, once relied upon to interpret management decisions and create meaning in the transforming workplace, were let go. Those who remained often manifested physical symptoms. Insomnia, high blood pressure, nausea, and depression have been cited as frequent reactions to unexpected and confusing changes within the workplace.

The corporate therapist can be useful in conducting both on- and off-site workshops to help employees cope with changes that have effected their departments and responsibilities. The abreaction of feelings associated with organizational change will decrease the tendency to somatize or turn to unhealthy forms of regression.

Corporate support groups that assist each other in adapting to the new workplace can be the foundation for better teamwork. As long as boundaries are enforced, the plant site or conference room venting session can relieve stress just by allowing its expression. Employees, now feeling better, become more receptive to empathizing with colleagues on team projects.

CORPORATE THERAPY AND THE
LOCAL BUSINESS COMMUNITY

The main reason for my decision to leave URC in 1985 and form my own company was to minimize overnight travel. Management consultants routinely travel from Monday (or Sunday night) through Friday, week in and week out. As my husband and I had not seen very much of each other in five years, I was determined to settle down. I began approaching CEOs in and around Philadelphia so that I could continue my work and still be home each evening for dinner.

I was amazed to discover a receptive market for CDM's services among several local prominent CEOs. As they all knew each other, I quickly established a CEO referral network. I found my business grew by word of mouth and confidential referral. Like a neighborhood physician, I was called upon to assist local CEOs who were in the throes of organizational transformation.

To meet nonreferred CEO prospects, I generally sent a personal letter of introduction to their secretary or chief administrative assistant. I had learned how powerful these gatekeepers were in screening solicitors and championing worthwhile resources. To meet them, I held a free stress management workshop. After having established credibility, I was given many first appointments with their chief executive bosses.

My alternative approach for impossible-to-meet CEOs was to engage local "power brokers." These were executives who personally interacted with CEOs on social or business matters. After having explained CDM's vision, I contracted formally with them for paid introductions. Over the years, I have found this approach to be an efficient and effective method of meeting new clients when I do not have a track record in a particular industry or country.

Power brokers are often retired board members, former chief executives and other well-established professionals who do not have a conflict of interest in making a specific referral. Fees can range from a one-time flat charge for a first appointment, to a percentage of a consultancy contract, depending upon involvement in the sales and delivery processes.

You will find, as I did, that many power brokers are responsive to an initial meeting. This typically entails a formal presentation in order to learn about your services. You can then explore together whether an arrangement is possible. I have found that most social and business networking is unnecessary and unproductive. If you can secure a personal introduction to a potential client in his or her office, why waste the time?

TRANSFORMING THE ORGANIZATION MEANS TRANSFORMING THE PEOPLE

If your goal is to accomplish transformation, then your work must start at the top of your client's organization. There are worthwhile consulting projects at every level of a corporation, but systemic change must be driven top-down.

Many psychotherapists in private practice who are graduates of CDM's corporate therapy seminars have told me how surprised they are when a private executive client reports how much he is modeling what he has learned in his day-to-day work environment. These clinicians are often asked to make a corporate call in order to bring others up to speed.

In essence, this is the nature of corporate therapy: A critical mass of leadership engages in accelerated self-growth work facilitated by a corporate therapist. The CEO and his team promote and model new values and behaviors. Extremely challenging growth goals are agreed upon. The system is then sufficiently energized to break through its homeostasis. Businesses processes are redesigned to support this new accelerated growth rate.

When transformation occurs over time and achieves developmental milestones, the organization will never regress to its former state. It will have setbacks similar to those experienced by individual clients in private practice. It will also have to respond to unanticipated external forces, such as a major legislative change. However, the self-awareness gained through therapeutically-oriented individual work, coupled with teambuilding and other group events, ensures a fundamental shift in individual and group consciousness. From this shift, better performance will emanate.

Throughout my practice, I have seen the awareness and acceptance of psychotherapeutic interventions grow within my own client's organizations as well in the corporate world overall. It is becoming quite fashionable to have a "shrink" on retainer, along with other must-haves of the twenty-first century, including a personal trainer, psychic advisor, and plastic surgeon!

4

Psychology as Technology in the Workplace

With the wizardry of computer technology providing and processing information faster than the left brain can absorb it, we are quickly evolving into a right-brain-dominant society. What does this mean? We will come to rely more on intuition, symbolism, and sensation than logic, reason, and analysis. In this "information overload" environment, our ability to use "gut feelings" and intimacy as decision-making tools will increase. Our skills in the emotional arena will need to become considerably more sophisticated as well.

Changes in the way we process information and make decisions are dramatic in and of themselves. When combined with the current demand to adapt to rapid change, psychology becomes an effective technology for achieving ongoing adaptation in the workplace.

This evolution affects all levels of an organization. In addition to becoming more flexible to new opportunities, roles, and responsibilities, employees will have to become independent and self-reliant. Rather than seeking approval from symbolic parental authority figures, work teams will be more autonomous. This will require substantial emotional growth. Psychotherapeutic support will be needed until functioning without a safety net is comfortable.

This is what is needed by the survivors; in this Darwinian business climate, only the strongest and most politically astute will survive.

Those abandoned are enraged, humiliated, and debilitated for a while, some permanently.[1] They need psychotherapeutic support as well.

The people left behind to fulfill the corporate vision are as diverse in nature and personality as the organizations that they work in. Together, they and their organization weave a complex fabric of history, values, motives, emotions, and interactions, making it impossible to separate the psyche from the system, the past from the present, needs from goals, and intentions from outcomes. In the following three CDM case studies taken from our mentoring programs, you will see the role of psychology as a technology for understanding and intervening in the dance between the organization and employee, between the system and psyche.

Case Study 1

Tom and the American Dream [2]

Tom Dawson joined ALM corporation right out of college as a supervisor in the machine shop. Over the next 10 years, he was assigned to several cost centers. These provided him with managerial experience, as well as an overview of the production processes from Order Entry to Final Test and Pack.

Tom was aggressive in promoting innovations. He streamlined the manufacturing process and reduced the unit cost of the product. By age 34, his efforts were rewarded. He was transferred to corporate headquarters as Director of Quality Assurance. As a senior executive reporting to the CEO, he was responsible for creating corporate policy on quality, as well as standardizing quality practices worldwide. In his new role, he was also a member of the Executive and Finance committees. It was widely believed, as the youngest senior executive ever at ALM, he stood a good chance of becoming the CEO himself one day.

Tom excelled at being responsible; in fact, he was trained since birth to worry about and take charge of others. His father had left home before he was three; his mother worked full-time to support Tom and his two younger sisters. As soon as he could ride a bike, he found a series of jobs that kept him busy until and throughout college. He married young as well, choosing a wife with serious ambitions of her own. During his early career, he sacrificed to support her through school as well as to establish her private medical practice. Now with

---

[1] Harry Levinson. "What Killed Bob Lyons?" *Harvard Business Review*, 1963.
[2] Names are fictitious, although the cases are real.

two kids, Tom was even more determined to succeed. Yet, within a year of his promotion there was talk of a transfer—or worse. To many, the sudden reversal in his popularity was a mystery. To others, it was simply the company's culture of "here today, gone tomorrow; everyone is expendable."

But what was really happening to Tom? We'll examine his predicament shortly. Right now, let's look at another common corporate dilemma.

Case Study 2

Randall Pauley: Solid Citizen and CEO

Randall is Chief Executive of Normar, an international engineering services firm in the utilities industry. In his 24-year tenure, he has built new divisions and established new markets. Randall patented technology that has given Normar a competitive advantage as well. Now, in this new, more competitive climate, he must convince his 5,000 plus managers and 60,000 employees to eliminate the costly bureaucracy that has metastasized throughout the organization.

As he tours facilities, Randall is stunned by the sluggish pace and lack of momentum driving day-to-day operations. Morale is low and job security is uncertain. In response, Randall initiates a series of town-hall meetings. He tries to energize his management toward a future new vision of a leaner, more aggressive Normar.

At Randall's direction, a massive analysis and redesign of business processes is undertaken. Work teams are formed to improve efficiencies within divisions and between departments. An incentive program is launched to encourage the achievement of ambitious performance targets. Randall is careful to keep both the media and his Board abreast of his new initiatives. Both groups of stakeholders are confident that Normar will again be an organization on the move. Yet 24 months later, the numbers are further declining. Why?

Add Normar to the puzzle, and consider yet a third dilemma.

Case Study 3

Jimmy B.: The Golden Boy

Jimmy B. is the founder of LPN Systems, a fast-growing entrepreneurial software design firm. LPN has recently gone public, with staggering results. The business plan calls for continued growth through acquisitions and joint ventures. Jimmy B. is a favorite in the investment community. His high public profile and media image helps the stock to climb. Investment capital is his for the asking.

Jimmy makes a series of acquisitions designed to expand LPN's offering, increase marketshare, and establish a dominant industry position. Due diligence on the acquisitions is thorough; LPN can afford to be discerning. Each purchase is accompanied by the expected media and promotional hoopla. The stock continues to climb.

Four years later, LPN is on the verge of bankruptcy. It has shrunk to one-fifth of its maximum size. Stock has plummeted. Jimmy has forfeited the jet fleet and several of his personal assets. The media struggles to interpret the rise and fall of LPN. Undaunted, Jimmy promises his comeback will be even more spectacular the second time around but the investment community is disillusioned. What took the shine out of Jimmy's rising star?

What went wrong for each of these executives and the corporations in which they became hopelessly entwined?

You might have guessed that in each of these case studies, a thorough knowledge of business will not be enough to understand what essentially went wrong. While the business community and popular media thrive on such predicaments and their subsequent dissection, one cannot fully appreciate the full reality of what happened without an understanding of psychology.

However, with psychological intervention these outcomes could have been effected, or at least predicted.

THE CASE OF TOM: THE PARENTIFIED CHILD

In the case of Tom, his predisposition to being "parentified" led to a complex and fatal role reversal with his boss, the chief executive. Without a strong internalized father introject, Tom eagerly sought the approval and acceptance of his older male colleagues. He soon took on responsibilities far beyond his experience and functional expertise. He further positioned himself as the confidante and caretaker of his boss, a newly appointed CEO with fears of failure. In an unconscious compulsive repetition of the symbiotic bond formed early with his mother, in which they were "two against the world," Tom "organized" his boss to become emotionally dependent on him. Tom's fantasy to rescue the corporation from a history of bad decisions could never be fulfilled. Neither could he have rescued his mother at an earlier time. Trapped unconsciously in his past, his grandiosity and desperate need for fathering heightened by the anxieties of his promotion, caused him to plunge headfirst into a dynamic from which he could not recover.

As expected, Tom's older colleagues, jealous of his quick assent, colluded to see him fail. His boss, once enchanted by Tom's vision and strength of conviction, became disillusioned when the promised bottomline results were not forthcoming. What was once a mutually satisfying but highly dangerous intimacy, regressed into a series of frosty confrontations. Tom responded alternately by withdrawing into a severe depression and charging back with enraged accusations of exploitation and betrayal. The relationship became unbearable for both. As Tom's utility declined, his peers escalated their scapegoating tactics. Essentially, Tom was abandoned by both his colleagues and boss.

Finally overwhelmed by the tidal wave of disappointment rushing over him, Tom physically and emotionally collapsed. While he was kept on the payroll until his physical recovery, his image at ALM was permanently scarred. His wife and mother were stunned by this outcome but supportive of Tom's decision to leave. It was so unlike Tom to walk out or fail, they thought. He had always been so responsible.

RANDALL: THE KEEPER OF ILLUSIONS

Conversely, Randall P. of Normar had a rather uneventful childhood. His career unfolded in a steady upward climb to the top of his organization. A practical and pragmatic man, he believed that hard work and sensible actions would produce expected results. An engineer by training, he scoffed at the notion that the "softer" social sciences, like psychology, could provide him with important strategic input. However, he took great pride in implementing the very latest business practices. He often used consultants to supply him with new ideas and techniques. When Normar failed to deliver results, no one was more surprised than he. Randall thought he did everything right; just like the experts said, and just like the examples in the popular management books.

While Randall's childhood and company politics provided him with stability and security, he lacked the necessary hypervigilance and antennae to accurately assess Normar's real progress. The youngest of nine, he learned early to buckle down to work. Therefore, the reaction of his organization to create illusions about performance and conceal its deeper problems (a typical dynamic in all transformations) was significantly increased. Further, Randall was not schooled in the dynamics of transformation, and how to predict and manage its progressive and regressive oscillations. By not taking a systemic approach, Randall set himself up as a victim of the "Ghandi effect," a dynamic in which the organization bipolarizes into subfactions to maintain its homeostasis, or ceiling limit on growth.

In Randall's world, saboteurs could flourish by undermining the momentum of his change program. In his naiveté and denial, Randall did not see how often he was duped. For Randall, the first step toward the true transformation of Normar would require that he become a student of the transformation process. He would have to accept both systemic principles and psychological realities, then integrate these into his strategic business plan. He would also have to face the abandonment he felt within his family that caused him to retreat into himself at an early age.

The second step for Randall would be far more difficult. He would have to learn to empathize with the people whose role and identities were changing along with Normar's direction. This would require that he relate to his people in a more intimate, supportive way. To do this, he would have to embark on his own self transformation journey. Only then, would the Ghandi effect be arrested, and the homeostasis within his organization overcome.

JIMMY P.: CHRIST FIGURE OR SATAN HIMSELF?

Jimmy P. of LPN might be accurately labeled a narcissist by a clinician with a trained eye. His attractiveness, charisma, grandiosity, and craving for attention would be obvious clues. A clinician might also have predicted that a strong probability existed for him to lead LPN on a roller coaster ride to *hell*. However, the powers of seduction resplendent in the narcissistically disturbed character[3] are not wasted on the corporate community, as it thrives as much on image as substance.

After a scrupulous investigation into Jimmy's illustrious Ivy League past, a layman still would be unable to predict that his lack of self-love would prohibit him from allowing LPN to succeed. As a result, his grandiose visions would be ignored by the executives of his newly acquired companies. His need to dominate and control discussions,

---

[3] Alice Miller, *The Drama of the Gifted Child*. (New York: Basic Books, 1981).

rather than listen and gather data, would create serious gaps in his understanding of their changing businesses. Any executive who dared to challenge his direction would be viewed as either a competitor or enemy, dangerous and expendable.

For Jimmy B., with a buried history of emotional abuse and failed business schemes, sufficient insight is unlikely. He does not have enough selfhood to face the shame, humiliation, and self-hatred that lurks behind his narcissistic defense.

Hence, a more appropriate intervention for organizations plagued with chief executives like LPN, is to resurrect the careers and businesses routinely destroyed by such characterologically dysfunctional leaders. They leave thousands in their midst wondering what went wrong.

In my own corporate therapy practice, I have encountered these three character types—the parentified child, the schizoid, and the narcissist—many times. In each case, the transformation of the chief executive was required in order to transform the organization's culture. I have also worked with many relatively healthy and mature chief executives. I have found a quick way to assess their emotional health is to ask them why their organization is underperforming. If they respond in a way that acknowledges their own responsibility for leadership, they are an excellent candidate for culture transformation. When they project blame onto the organization, it is often indicative of the need for much deeper self-awareness first.

This next case, which illustrates the treatment of a borderline CEO with a history of incest, tested virtually all of my skills. Yet, I found that such a difficult case accelerated my own growth tremendously. While many clinicians find it hard to believe that a borderline personality is capable of rising to the chief executive level, the tremendous drive for achievement and need for attention among borderlines makes the executive suite a highly attractive pursuit.

ROBERT GROWS UP (AGAIN)

Robert started in the marketing department of a Fortune 500 organization that manufactures computer products. He rose quickly through the ranks by political savvy, hard work, and know how. He became the protege of the heir apparent to the chief executive officer. Well positioned for promotion, Robert was 48 years old when he was appointed

CEO. At 52, he became the chairman as well. With this achievement, he became one of the youngest Fortune 500 chairman in the nation, therefore actualizing his lifelong dream.

Robert's leadership abilities were tested when rising interest rates and heightened global competition forced him to close plants, down-size, and sell assets to shore up the company's bottomline. When he could find no other shortcuts, Robert was forced to seek new methods in order to restore his organization's competitive advantage. To Robert, failure of any kind represented death and disaster. He was determined to do whatever it took to succeed.

I was contacted by Robert's best friend, another CDM chief executive client, who told me that Robert was depressed and frightened of losing his job. My client warned me, "Iris, I don't know if you are up for this guy—everyone around him has ulcers."

I met Robert for lunch in his office. He was initially quite charming and eager for help. We agreed to work together on his "leadership development" once a week for half-day sessions. After completing his developmental history—which we at CDM call the "Success Interview" that looks at a chronology of successes from the earliest childhood memory to the present in order to understand core strengths—we focused on his family history.

Robert was an only child. He had been raised in a small town by an alcoholic father and sexually frustrated mother. Robert was the glue that kept the couple together. Their repetitive marital pattern focused on the father's physical abuse of his wife and her subsequent threats of adultery as retaliation for his mistreatment. Instead of turning to other men to spite her husband, she turned to Robert for comfort. She began an incestuous relationship with him when he was four that lasted until his early adolescence.

Executive men will often react to emotional disorders by immersing themselves in highly demanding intellectual pursuits. This can be a short-lived successful defense against conflicts and pain. Robert was no exception. He became an overachiever and excelled academically. School also provided an adaptive escape from his nightmare at home. He had no power to fix his family dynamics or even truly escape them. Doing well provided Robert with a means of attracting and pleasing substitute fantasy parents in the academic world, who untainted, could be internalized as healthy role models. This unconscious strategy protected him from hopelessness and ensured his ultimate survival.

As one might expect under these circumstances, Robert dated very little. When he married, he chose a woman with predictable dynamics.

She was quite wealthy; therefore perceived by him as not needy. She was also emotionally and sexually withholding. Unconsciously, this provided relief for both Robert's entrapment and engulfment terrors. As a result of their emotional blueprints, Robert and his wife formed a rigid marital contract. They made no sexual demands upon each other except to have children as necessary symbols of family life. The couple also maintained the emotional distance needed for Robert to focus solely on his work. While his wife sublimated her emotional needs in raising children, Robert ruthlessly pursued his dream of becoming a chief executive as quickly as possible. He often traveled for weeks at a time.

Robert's reputation in business was predictable as well. He was a difficult taskmaster; demanding, unyielding, distant, and hostile; yet when necessary, seductive and charming. He had no close corporate colleagues. His various secretaries typically sought psychotherapy to tolerate him. Not surprisingly, Robert showed general disdain for females. An obstructionist when it came to promoting them, he did not mince words while criticizing them. Minor performance problems often triggered full-blown rage.

He regularly sparred with his senior executives as well. Competitive and defiant, he maintained argumentative and confrontational relationships and showed little ability in building a team. His promotions were typically earned by his brilliance in creating solutions for various marketing or manufacturing crises. His ability to inspire and lead was often in question.

Robert's attitude toward his senior executives did little to encourage honesty and integrity among them. Because he was feared, they resorted to withholding valuable information from him. As the business declined, they knew it before he did. When I arrived on the scene, operations was in trouble, and everyone was afraid to tell Robert. Typically, in a huge corporation such as his, it may often take as long as nine months for a cancer in operations to impact the bottomline. His direct reports, relieved that he was seeking help, confided the true realities of the business to me, hoping that I would communicate them to Robert in time for a turnaround.

When I began working with Robert, I utilized the principles of comprehensive family therapy[4] in the design of his treatment plan. His

---

[4] S. Kirschner and D. Kirschner, *Comprehensive Family Therapy: An Integration of Systemic and Intrapsychic Treatment Models.* (New York: Brunner/Mazel, 1986). This book is being reissued by John Wiley & Sons (New York) in 1996 as *Comprehensive Therapy of Couples and Families.*

current etiology was examined within a multigenerational context. Utilizing CDM's "Levels of Self" model, (see page 140, Figure 13.1) I mapped his core strengths, dynamics, and barriers. Given the nature of his childhood abuse, my therapeutic stance required both masculine and feminine inputs with extremely regulated distance and closeness. In order for healing to occur, Robert would need to consciously examine his childhood predicament, then experience the affect it created while in relationship to a trustworthy reparental agent. I would need to be fully prepared to be the object of his rage in the development of his transference.[5]

As his travel schedule demanded, much of this work was done in his own office. This added to the difficulty of increasing self-awareness, as the recall of significant trauma was involved. We found that weekend sessions were required in order for Robert to get in touch with his memories and feelings. Overall, his work with me took over three years.

In facilitating regression, one of the tools used was hypnosis. Through it, we returned to his earliest abusive episodes and re-experienced them together. Then we moved forward through his childhood, replacing painful memories with healing imagery.

Not surprisingly, underneath his terror, Robert was starved for emotional nurturance. At the outset of therapy, he was resistant to any intimate contact with his wife. As she became my ally in the treatment process, he was able to make significant strides in bonding her. She, of course, had to confront the origins of her own terrors of engulfment and annihilation, which kept her stuck in their old emotional dance. For over two years, the three of us met weekly at their home. This couple's work led to a dramatic shift in their marriage; which in turn, helped transform Robert's leadership of his team. Another family therapist was retained to assist their children.

To counterbalance the regressive nature of this therapeutic work, I introduced a progressive task into each session. To get Robert in touch with his business problems, I encouraged him to use intimacy as a communication strategy to uncover performance barriers that had been camouflaged.

As Robert healed, he began rethinking what he wanted to accomplish for himself and the corporation. He found that he now wanted to mentor, rather than annihilate his executives. This change in his style

---

[5] C. Jung. *The Psychology of the Transference.* (Princeton: Bolinger, 1966).

helped them to become true champions of the vision. Willing to adopt a similar mentoring approach in other levels of the corporation, they retained CDM to deliver a corporate-wide mentoring program involving over five hundred managers. Teambuilding at the top three levels of management was facilitated by CDM consultants as well.

It has been my experience that significant growth beyond intrapsychic ceiling barriers generally includes taking two steps forward and one step back. As a result, I encourage executive mentees to telephone me once a day to process regressive feelings associated with progressive growth. This *rapprochement* helps them to consolidate new wins into permanent success patterns. Demanding short interval contact allows the pace of treatment to be significantly accelerated, and provides the corporate therapist with regular progress reports.

With regard to this case and many like it, it is not uncommon for executive overachievers to find themselves stuck when the demands of a new role strain their defenses. In order to succeed, emotional work of this nature is often required. Yet, most chief and senior executives do not have an opportunity in the work environment to address this need for growth. Vulnerability could endanger their current position and jeopardize their future potential. Corporate therapy may be the only vehicle possible to get healing, as they may often be reluctant to seek private help.

5

The Self-Transformation Journey of Corporate Executives

My chief executive clients are great skiers, golfers, tennis players and devoted family men—in addition to being true masters of change. While I admire and cheer them on, I wouldn't want their jobs because they include some truly wrenching tasks. They must fire their friends, close down branches; divest plants; hold their temper with parasitic reporters who are crucifying them; second-guess unsupportive board members; endure endless business dinners; give countless speeches about a vision for the future; sit in constant meetings: selling, persuading, cajoling, scolding—finally threatening—noncommittal managers to live the corporate vision in practice.

They do this with the full awareness that their job actually affords them little direct power. Virtually every goal they have must be implemented through others. The emotional resilience and sophistication required to be successful in this role are enormous.

Fortune 500 chief executives that I've known are running organizations as large and complex as small countries. Often the barriers they face daily include slashed budgets, shrunken markets, ruthless competitors, higher costs, resentful employees, impatient boards, disloyal executives and frustrated customers. The average tenure of a Fortune 500 chief executive today is less than five years. This trend brings new meaning to the concept of early retirement. Currently, the United

States is filled with homeless corporate soldiers who lost the war on profits and productivity.

Observing CEOs in action, I often have wondered whether it is fair to assume that one executive alone can do this job. Can anyone be this much of a miracle worker, messiah, maverick and maniac? Should we keep featuring CEOs on the covers of magazines, poised behind the antique desk or in front of the company jet, immaculately dressed, exuding courage, charisma and conviction? Or are we prepared to go beyond our illusion of leaders? Masterminding the resurrection of prosperity in the 1990s and into the next century requires a realistic appraisal of the role of corporate leader, as well as that of a management team.

In our times, it takes a particular kind of corporate hero to steer the ship, as well as a particular level of team process. When I began CDM in 1985, I found that Chief Executives intuitively grasped the enormous power of psychology. Its potential application was viewed not as a clinical science, but as a technology of understanding and accelerating growth; transforming perceptions and belief systems; unlocking creativity, motivation and commitment; healing the organization's grief from change and loss; and most importantly, predicting the future behavior of individuals and groups based upon their past. For example, if every chief executive understood the impact of bipolarity in transforming cultures, many might still have jobs today. If board directors and regulators understood the profound role that character plays in decisionmaking, then many organizations might not be in crisis. Psychology provides insights critical for leadership and success in these incredibly challenging times.

CDM assists chief executives accelerate their growth and the growth of their management through applying systemic and intrapsychic principles to managing change.

We architect with our clients a relationship-driven culture that rewards commitment, excellence and that terrible "I" word—intimacy. No, I don't mean executives holding hands and chanting in a candlelit swimming pool, bungie jumping with customers, or going on wilderness walks to find the hidden warrior within. Instead, we define intimacy operationally as the capacity within an organization to seek the truth and to insist on accurate, unfiltered data about its business and performance.

Data that is unfiltered, unpostured and unpositioned: free of distortions, projections, ambivalence, politics and illusions; which goes beyond one's own inevitable tendency to misperceive, misinterpret, misconstrue and essentially mislead—that is a true competitive advantage. When this begins with executives knowing themselves and their operations intimately and reflecting the reality that surrounds them, the organization can truly transform. This also requires a recognition that those at the top are incredibly vulnerable. The corporate jet, limousine, board memberships, and private clubs are not adequate protection today against a couple of quarters of bad numbers.

In the *Hero with a Thousand Faces* Joseph Campbell,[1] the mythologist who seeks to define fundamental similarities among religions and cultures worldwide, elegantly describes the ultimate challenge facing most world-class corporations today: to find heroes, then convince them to take an unknown uncharted journey beyond the self and the organization as they know it. He aptly terms this journey as "entering the belly of the whale." Heroes are those who answer the "call to action." Their journey as he describes it, is dark and perilous, fraught with danger and disaster. There are life-threatening tests the hero must pass in order to receive his boon. In the world beyond the year 2000, the boon may very well be as anticlimactic as corporate survival itself.

During his journey, the hero is assisted by mysterious helpers and mystical spirits. These powerful entities support him in surpassing his tests. The journey itself is hell-raising and death-defying as well as miraculous and glorious. It is all-encompassing, haunting both the hero's waking and sleeping consciousness. At each juncture or impasse, he doesn't know if he will succeed. Like doing business in the 1990s, there are no guarantees.

Essentially, CDM leads the chief executive and his heroes on the journey to self-transformation from being an organization rooted in history, tradition, glory, rhetoric, false security, illusion and repetition—into becoming a self-transmuting system able to envision and accomplish ongoing quantum leaps in growth.

The hero's journey is not for every executive. It requires a steadfast commitment, regardless of budgets, downturns, and other economic and external distractions. The journey also requires a leap of faith. It takes knowing that the only true path to transformation is within the self of the executive. It also takes emotional fortitude, an affinity for risk-taking and an embracement of fear and anxiety. The hero must

---

[1] Joseph Campbell, *Hero with a Thousand Faces*, (Princeton, NJ: Princeton University, 1949).

have the deepest belief in the invisible intangible forces that shape his consciousness.

It is within the rich, unexplored, often disregarded interior terrain that the potential for transformation is discovered. *[The hidden self within the executive hero contains the seeds for ongoing mastery of the business, family, body, and spirit. Becoming acquainted and aligned with this self and its various aspects and talents, is the single most essential activity for preparing future executives for leadership in the next century.]*

Eastern cultures have long accepted that peak performance is a function of the balancing of forces within the self. It has taken Western corporations literally the threat of annihilation to abandon the sequential approach and think systemically. This transition is nothing short of a revolution, requiring the reorientation and reprogramming of countless corporate heroes.

As Campbell describes it, the assistance of an inspirational guide is central to the transformation journey. In fact, all disciplines of psychology describe growth as occurring within the context of a significant relationship. The role of this significant other is to provide the inspiration, grounding and belief in the vision and potential of the hero. In fact, the guide must believe in the hero with far more conviction, determination, and passion than the hero can muster up for himself.

In the culture transformation journey, each hero is supplied with a CDM mentor who catalyzes the hero's self-transformation. The mentor provides both direction and support throughout the hero's journey. In order for culture transformation to occur, a critical mass of heroes at all levels must be simultaneously engaged. The mentoring of multi-levels of hero executives leads to an organized systemic transformation of the culture.

On a systemic level, groups of heroes come together with peers, staffs, and mentors to transform business symbols including strategies, processes, meetings, and relationships. A style of debate and confrontation is encouraged to tear through the old reality. As part of this process, a commitment to insist on accurate data about the business and culture is made.

Engineering the transformation of a culture is a process of managing accelerated growth. The difference between growth and transformation is a matter of degree. Transformation occurs when the vision or growth goal exceeds the capacity to tolerate growth, at approximately 45 percent over historical performance. This "stretch" provides the momentum to seek adaptation at an entirely new level, thus creating a breakthrough. While traditional change management models yield short-term improvement, transformation ensures against the long-term dangers of backsliding. Transformation accelerates growth as a strategic business process that can be measured by bottomline results.

In CDM's model, transformation is defined in two ways:

1. *The depth of self awareness:* As the growth goal increases, awareness and self-consciousness must deepen in order to manage the regressive trends that occur. These include: moving beyond one's illusions about oneself and one's potential, moving beyond the defenses that protect the self from the anxieties of growth; examining and resolving the underlying ambivalence that prevents a total commitment to achieving one's vision; embracing fears and terrors associated with failure and success including shame and abandonment; and ultimately, discovering one's will—an energy source that can fuel the activation and achievement of any vision. Each phase of mentoring corresponds to a stage of growth required for successful self- and culture transformation.

2. *Strategic management of the growth dynamic:* In systemic transformation the process and dynamics of growth include:

   o A progressive/regressive oscillation. As the stretch factor increases, the pull to return to status quo performance or even self destruction, increases as well. Arthur Stein (1980) originally termed this dynamic "PAR" or Progressive Abreactive Regression. In working with the Kirschners[2] on a corporate application of PAR, CDM charted predictable regressions that must be optimally resolved to sustain and increase progressions in corporate performance. (See Chapter 13.) Completing a full transformation cycle takes between two and three years, based upon the emotional resilience of the clients.

   o The phenomenon of bipolarity, as originally described by Bennis and Shephard[3] in their theory of group develop-

---

[2] For a full description of this model, see S. Kirschner and D. Kirschner. *Comprehensive Family Therapy.* (New York: John Wiley & Sons, 1996).
[3] W. Bennis and H. Shephard. A *Theory of Group Development. Human Relations,* 9, 415–437, 1956.

ment. Through conducting and observing groups in which the facilitator strategically refused to direct the group, Bennis and Shepard outlined an evolutionary process occurring over two phases. With the absence of leader input, the group bipolarizes into subfactions representing members orientation to power and authority and intimacy and dependence, respectively. In the first phase, the subgroup oriented toward power assumes the leadership of the group. In the second phase, the group struggles with its needs for intimacy. Ultimately, it recognizes that its purpose, dilemma, and situation must dictate the use of power, as well as the boundaries and relationships within the group.

Cultures undergoing transformation initially behave much like a "leaderless" group. There is uncertainty and anxiety in reaction to the CEO's intention for transformation. Subgroups of the transforming culture bipolarize into regenerative and destructive camps. If the destructive group is not managed strategically, it will attempt to destroy the system. CEO's not trained in psychological models of group process underestimated the inevitability and power of this dynamic. As a result, many attempts at culture transformation in the 1980s failed.

- The dynamics of death[4] and rebirth. Transformation requires a new way of perceiving the self, the system and the world. "Death" of the old self creates the space for rebirth. This process includes both grief and rejuvenation in order for the new identity to be integrated. As a result, there is temporary dependence upon the mentor.

- Finally, a new and strong foundation must be built to ensure the potential for ongoing transformation. New insights, beliefs, practices, and self-structures are created along the way. Part of building this foundation is done by reflecting upon the transformation journey. Observing one's experiences and abreacting various feelings to the mentor helps integrate learning.

---

[4] Elizabeth Kübler-Ross. *Stages of Death and Dying.* (New York: Macmillan Publishing Co., Inc., 1970).

During the executive hero's journey, he is led by his CDM mentor through five developmental phases of self transformation. Successive resolution of each are critical to the success of his overall journey. (Simultaneously, the culture as a system moves through phases of growth, detailed in Chapter 11 as does the mentoring interpersonal dynamic, outlined in Chapter 13.)

PHASE ONE: GROUNDING IN SUCCESS

The first task of transformation is to create the context in which transformation can occur. For most of us, our lifetime of successes are discounted. Instead, disappointments and failures haunt our consciousness. These internal interferences must be eliminated before transformation can begin. Through a proprietary CDM process (detailed on page 70), each executive hero is led through a chronological review of past successes and a process for integrating them into a platform for accelerated growth. Then each hero builds the optimal environment for creating future success at work and at home. This becomes the "winning formula" for proactively managing the self transformation process.

PHASE TWO: THE STRETCH

While visions are promoted in most organizations and in the media, few people including executives understand the process for accessing parts of the self where visions are created and realized. As a result, the hero is taught how to envision mastery in the arenas of work, family life, sports and health. This "four quadrant" approach ensures there is sufficient pressure on all sides to catalyze transformation.

For each quadrant vision, a stretch goal of 45 percent over historical annual performance is mandatory. Why? Consider the result that is achieved from becoming a triathlete. It is far better than the result achieved from merely "getting in shape." It is this stretch factor that activates the dynamics of transformation and ensures the breakthrough.

PHASE THREE: THE WALL

There comes a time in which self-destruction is favored over the impending death of the old self. Yet, the "roller coaster ride to hell" must be cleverly avoided. The longing to flameout or give up is incredibly high even with proper support. At some point in the transformation journey, each executive hero hits this "wall." He is expected to ascend it, with the help of his mentor.

The wall is a metaphor for the gatekeeper of the hidden self. The wall consists of the negative beliefs, messages and experiences internalized in childhood before each hero had the psychological defenses to deflect negativity. The wall must be artfully overcome.

We have only to look as far as world-class athletes to observe the process of breaking through the wall within the realm of a relationship. Through years of intensive coaching they have internalized strategies for self-mobilizing, thus transcending what appeared moments before to be certain defeat.

The executive hero learns the art of "strategic regression" as a reliable way of moving through the wall. He abreacts his internal battle between the old and new selves to his mentor. In this rapprochement, sufficient energy and inspiration are introjected to dissolve negative introjects.

PHASE FOUR: THE HELL

As if the wall isn't enough of a test, the hero must then encounter his inner demons as he travels through "the midnight of the soul." He experiences waves of apathy, terrors of annihilation, deep grief and longing for the past. His old limited self is dying. Yet, this death is neither quick nor painless. The new self sees and senses the world in a totally different way. The hero even with support experiences almost unbearable isolation. His world is in turmoil as beliefs, expectations, and relationships are rapidly changing. The mentor assists the hero creates a new world to support his new powerful self. In the process, the hero's confidence soars. He has endured. The karmic debt for learning the secret of transformation is paid.

PHASE FIVE: THE WIN

The hero, quite by surprise, suddenly experiences himself at the top of his own mountain. And contrary to popular mythology, he is not lonely at the top. He celebrates his successful transformation with his mentor, corporate colleagues and family members.

Privately, the hero reflects on the series of defeats and victories that have led to his ultimate win. He has earned his boon. He realizes that transformation is not a myth nor mystery. It is a process. He re-enters the world wiser and willing to guide the transformation of others. As a guide in his own right, he no longer needs his mentor. However, he knows intuitively that help will always be available. When the student is ready, the teacher will reliably appear.

Not all executive heroes are cut out for this journey. I have found that there is a 20-60-20 rule regarding the transformation of executives. Twenty percent become champions of change, true growth junkies at heart. Sixty percent transform with mentoring. Twenty percent typically self-select out. They are unable to grow into the demands of the transforming culture.

Knowing this rule to be fairly consistent, however, does not allow for predicting successes and failures upfront. All of the chief executive's heroes must be given equal opportunity to transform, as well as a roadmap and a skillful guide. It is often quite surprising who rises to the occasion and who chooses to move on. Very often, those executives labeled as "dead wood" have been some of our most accomplished mentees.

In this chapter, I have illustrated for you the journey that is required for executives to transform their organizations into the next century. Because it is psychological in nature, it requires a trained psychotherapist to act as a guide and mentor.

In the next section, we will turn our attention back to *your* own journey from couch to corporation. One cannot help another transform until one has transformed oneself!

PART TWO

On Becoming a
Corporate Therapist

6

Your Couch-to-Corporation Transformation

Preparing yourself for becoming a corporate therapist requires nothing short of your own personal transformation. It begins with the way you currently perceive the practice of psychotherapy and how it differs when applied within the corporation.

There are certain principles that can guide your transition from couch to corporation. For example, corporate therapy is essentially teaching an organization how to positively master change at all levels—systemic, strategic, structural, interpersonal, and intrapsychic—in response to a shift in vision or direction. Further, corporate therapy can assist an organization to transform itself from one stage of the corporate life cycle to another in a way that will increase its competitive advantage.

THE DIFFERENCES BETWEEN CORPORATE AND PRIVATE THERAPY

The differences between corporate therapy and private therapy are distinct. A major difference between the two is that in private therapy, greater emphasis is generally placed on identifying the historical, intrapsychic origin of the "presenting" problem. In the business world, however, corporate therapists often may limit talking about family history, as it promotes regressive behavior in the workplace. Instead of helping executives deal with past issues, you will be focusing them on

47

recognizing the forces that are affecting them now in the marketplace, within the business and within themselves. In special cases, you might choose to focus on the childhood of the chief executive if he is the "authorizing" mentee client.

Another difference between the couch and the corporation, is the context created by staying in the office versus going on-site. Private therapy occurs typically in weekly one hour intervals within the confines of your office. When time is not a factor, therapy may last until the envisioned result is achieved or the client is weaned away from the therapist.

Corporate therapy is done exclusively on-site in the client executive's office. If the CEO is the authorizing client, he or she will select the criteria for participant inclusion and the business focus. Typical goals are change management and performance improvement. Results may be measured utilizing current indices or created especially for the program. Also, time is of the essence. Sessions may run several times a week or over marathon-type weekends. Therefore a highly directive and strategic approach is taken, similar to short-term psychotherapy work. We at CDM describe our service as "engineered transformation for accelerating competitive advantage." This implies that once goals are set, we provide methodologies and techniques that direct the change process.

WHO IS BEST SUITED TO DO CORPORATE THERAPY

I am often asked what type of psychotherapist is best suited for this kind of work. To answer this, we must look at the corporation's needs to identify the optimal service provider.

Organizations operate simultaneously on many levels. They operate on a systemic level, as decisions being made change the fabric of the organization. They operate on a strategic level, as change impacts the direction. They operate on a structural level, as there is a reorganization of people's responsibilities and tasks. Changes on an operational level effect how work gets done, horizontally and vertically. As changes are introduced, functions are realigned to fulfill new roles. The operational level also unfolds intradepartmentally. On an interpersonal level, change affects the relationships of people who work together. They are affected on an intrapsychic level as well. As the organization is internalized as an object, the intrapsychic dynamics of the employee must shift in response.

Everything you do as a corporate therapist affects these levels simultaneously. You need to have broad psychotherapeutic training to keep track of the various rippling effects. Corporate therapists should have a background in family systems and group processes as well as basic training in object relations.

You will also need to be skilled in many psychotherapeutic tools; there is a role for all in various corporate interventions. You should have a grasp of developmental theories to recognize milestones and how to achieve them. You must know how to resolve the repetition compulsion that underlies emotional conflict in order to correct developmental arrests.

The broader your training, the better. While having a narrow specialty may have served you well clinically, it will greatly limit your effectiveness in the multidimensional practice of corporate therapy. If you are thinking about making this transition, assess your therapeutic strengths and weaknesses. Then examine your training, clinical experience, and the kinds of therapy work that you have done in the past.

If you have worked best with individuals, for example, there is a role for you as a mentor or performance coach in the corporate world. If most of your work has been with families or groups, there is a role in facilitating teams. If you are a neuropsychologist, there is a role for doing customer analysis work. You do not necessarily need to be a generalist if you are already a specialist. However, your foundation and focus is the framework against which you will assess a corporation's needs and design an appropriate intervention. Therefore, your offering must be limited to your strengths.

You will need to understand business and have some working knowledge of its mechanics and nuances. One of the things that intimidates psychotherapists is not having a business background. But if you have a Ph.D. or M.D., and have spent the better part of your adult life as a practitioner, you have already proven yourself adept at learning. You will be able to acquire the necessary business knowledge fairly quickly.

You will not have to return to school to take business courses. My own career is example enough of how clients will teach you their businesses. However, you should begin your education by reading popular business publications. Become aware of what is challenging the business world each day. Familiarize yourself with trends such as strategic planning, downsizing and process re-engineering. You can read the popular management books that have been published in the last ten years to get a genuine grip on why and how Corporate America evolved into its present state. (See "Bibliography" at the end of this book.)

Not only must you educate yourself about business trends, you will need to articulate them in the language in which business people communicate. The slang used in the corporate world symbolizes experience and understanding of basic business models. After working with you, your clients may start to incorporate your clinical vocabulary. However, in the beginning you will have to speak corporate lingo to build credibility. You need to dispel the myth that you are an "academic egghead" who lives in the world of ideas instead of the "real world" of business.

You can enhance your working knowledge of business by talking to friends who are corporate executives. Alert them of your plans so they know the specific type of information that you are seeking. The saying goes in the management consulting world that there are only five things to know about any one industry or corporation, as long as they are the right five things! Following that advice, much of my own education has come from business lunches or dinners. I often invite technical experts to address my questions and provide a reading list, while entertaining them at a special restaurant with a great wine list. Chief financial officers, investment bankers, attorneys, chief operating officers, and sales managers make effective business mentors.

CHALLENGES OF THE TRANSITION

The transition from private to corporate practice is not without challenges—the biggest is terror—not just fear, but absolute, unadulterated terror that stems from moving from a context in which you feel comfortable, into a foreign context with which you have little identification or familiarity.

This is not simply fear of failure. It is associated with changing your total identity. This transition challenges the psychotherapist's basic view of boundaries, assessment, treatment, and self presentation. It requires building a new identity without losing one's basic foundation. For example, in corporate therapy there is no role for formally diagnosing people. The transition also challenges the way that most clinicians see themselves. They must move from viewing themselves as healers to facilitators, mentors or coaches.

The level of exposure also differs greatly between private and corporate practice. In the corporate world, you will be asked to give executives input on problems they are having with staffs, customers, competitors, as well as themselves. The scope of your input may range from the shop floor to strategic business decisions. In addition to the time you spend on site, your corporate clients may also phone you on a scheduled basis. It may feel quite engulfing and it is more difficult to set boundaries. You must learn to say succinctly "It beats the hell out of me" when asked for advice in an area in which you are unqualified. Misleading a business client can be disastrous.

Another major challenge for psychotherapists is to create an actual consultancy. The consulting industry is unregulated and anyone can be a consultant if they have a product or service to market. Entry barriers are nonexistent and there are no industrywide guidelines for pricing services. There are no prescribed ethics that regulate the industry either. You need to consciously construct your own role, boundaries, approach and pricing based on your unique skills and target market.

HOW THE CONSULTING INDUSTRY WORKS

Consequently, the next step for the psychotherapist is to learn about the management consulting industry and how it operates. You will be approaching potential clients who have been hiring consultants for many years. If you are going to compete, you need to understand the consulting culture. You need to present yourself as a credible consultant as opposed to the "shrink" the typical executive perceives the psychotherapist to be. (See Required Reading.)

You will be competing for contracts with management consultants who are extremely comfortable in the business world. The library is a good place to start to research the consultants in your area and the services that they provide. And again, don't hesitate to turn to friends. Chances are they have dealt with management consultants or they know someone who is willing to share information with you.

You'll find that the reputation of the management consulting industry is generally poor. While there exists a handful of reputable firms who have consistently proven they add value, most corporate clients have horror stories to tell. Criticisms of consultancies include poor ethics and lack of confidentiality, simplistic analysis methods, poor implementation skills, and being unable to provide and measure results. By contrast, the ethics and boundaries that regulate the psychotherapy disciplines are viewed as a welcome relief.

Psychotherapists are also challenged to create a product line. You must be extremely specific about your offerings if you are going to compete. Understanding the corporate context plays a critical role in developing a proposal for services. It must be timely and address an urgent contemporary management problem.

Most domestic and international organizations are currently working on business and culture transformations. Within the transformation context, there are lots of ways the corporate therapist can intervene. You can offer a broad service which can be actual culture transformation, as CDM does. Or you can pick one of several specialties. You can help executives better understand their customers. You can teach them to use psychological methods to get a competitive advantage in developing new products or services, or marketing them in a way that is more appealing to customers. Therapists with a background in group therapy can focus on teambuilding, by helping managers work successfully in groups. Executive coaching or mentoring is an ideal service for psychotherapists to work one-on-one with executives leading and managing change.

Corporate therapists are also ideally suited for recruitment and screening services. They can utilize psychological models to help an organization identify who won't make it through a transformation. They can screen a short list of recommended potential hires. They can also help ease the trauma of downsizing. This can be extraordinarily rewarding work when therapeutic tools are used to help people heal from disengagement.

Psychotherapists turned corporate therapists need to develop their offering from a perspective of their strengths. Laying a foundation for a new career should be based on success from the past. It is better to narrow your offering to a few specific areas as too much, too soon will be overwhelming.

Identifying the services you are going to offer leads to the challenge of marketing your services. The corporate therapist has to figure out who the right people are, then sell himself, which is often considered terrifying. The marketing process is made more difficult as most business people want to make appointments with people they already know. The days of seeing someone without an introduction or other prior contact are over.

If you are starting your marketing process from scratch—as most new corporate therapists are—you may need to establish a small group of people who can make business introductions for you. These power brokers can serve as a bridge between you and potential corporate clients. They include lawyers, accountants, advertising executives, public relations specialists, retired corporate executives, and retired board members. Power brokers are not difficult to find. They sit on the boards of the opera, ballet, and various museums as well as on boards of public corporations.

A good way to start meeting power brokers in your local community is to write a letter of introduction. Tell them your background and describe cases that you have treated in your private practice. Talk about your areas of expertise to provide them with insight into who you are. Let them know that you want to work with corporations. Explain that you would like to know who they know in corporations that you can meet. You also want to discuss a financial arrangement that is most comfortable.

This is definitely the best kept secret in the industry, but it is how "cold" management consulting typically gets done. Once you have built a reputation as a corporate therapist, most of your work will come through referral, just as it did when you were in private practice. When you are starting out, however, you may need introducers to get an opportunity to make a first presentation.

It is crucial to know who consumers of consulting services are to avoid presenting yourself at the wrong level. Typically, in a small company (less than $50—100 million in revenues) the owner or Chief Executive is the authorized buyer. Within the Fortune 1000, however, those who have access to the "management services" budget (which funds consulting projects) are senior executives reporting directly to the chief executive. Therefore, calling on middle managers may be educational, but it won't get you paid work.

Corporate executives who retain consultants are quite sensitized to being asked the following direct questions:

- ○ Do you have a management services budget?

- ○ Are you authorized to engage my services?

- ○ How much of a budget do you anticipate targeting for these kinds of services this year?

This direct approach will help you realistically evaluate whether the prospective client is truly interested in your service offering.

In terms of marketing, your materials must define and position you as an organization consultant who is an advisor or facilitator to corporations. Your business cards, company names, sales materials and services need to be consistent with the fact that you are not operating as a psychotherapist in private practice.

Many psychotherapists who do corporate consulting have established two corporate identities because they maintain a psychotherapy practice and a corporate therapy practice. They may see individual clients at the office, but when they go on site as corporate consultants, their other identity takes over. Never should you confuse the marketplace regarding your role, identity, intentions, services and approach.

Ironically, the corporate therapist identity is paradoxically different from that of the private practitioner. Don't put Ph.D. on your business card! The "doctor" title is often viewed with a combination of fear and distrust by the business community. The image conjures up an academic rather than someone who can sit with an executive and pragmatically tackle business problems.

When you approach an organization, what you are selling has to meet the needs and criteria of that market. It is crucial that you package yourself based on language that the corporation uses. It is within the context of language that money is budgeted for consulting services. For example, if you present yourself as someone who works on change management, it easy for your prospect to check the budget and say, "Oh yes, we have a budget for that," or "We have a budget for team-building," or "We have a budget for customer care."

Other rules apply to corporate therapy. Some of these contrast starkly with rules that you have followed as a psychotherapist. In the private practice setting, a patient comes with free choice. He has a right to set the expectations for therapy and choose what he wants to focus on. The rules in the business world are different, however. Many people with whom corporate therapists work did not choose to be involved in the consulting project. They were, in fact, told by their boss that the organization is undergoing an exercise and they are expected to participate. Initially, there may be much resistance. The corporate therapist may have to work much harder at establishing bonded and trusting relationships with several levels of participants.

Confidentiality will prove to be extraordinarily helpful in your new field. People in the corporate world will be suspicious therefore careful of what they tell you. As a result, there is a need to explain confidentiality and how the psychological field views it. At CDM, we provide mentoring program participants with a legal confidentiality contract to sign, signed by the CEO, which clearly explains what is and is not considered confidential.

In our Corporate Therapy workshops, participants complete a "100-Day Plan" to jump-start their new career. Many of the activities listed in Figure 6.1 (see page 56) became part of their 100-day commitment.

Key Activity	M1	M2	M3	M4	M5	M6	M7	M8	M9	M10	M11	M12
Examination of Your Goals ◦ Kind of work you love ◦ Financial requirements ◦ Time available ◦ Travel time available ◦ Time for transition	X											
Assess Your Strengths ◦ Key successes ◦ Lifetime successes ◦ Best clinical skills ◦ Other skills	X											
Research Consulting Industry ◦ Library research ◦ Talk to friends ◦ Interview consultants		X										
Create Your Vision ◦ Interview family members ◦ Financial implications ◦ Transition plan ◦ 1–3 year goals			X									
Develop Your Product Line ◦ Culture transformation ◦ Mentoring ◦ Customer analysis ◦ Culture analysis ◦ Out placement ◦ Recruiting/screening ◦ Other				X	X							
Target Your Market ◦ Industries ◦ Geography ◦ Client type ◦ Prospect list ◦ Contact list						X						
Position/Package Yourself ◦ Logo/tag ◦ Business cards ◦ Presentation kit ◦ Stationery ◦ Legal/accounting set up							X	X				
Marketing/Sales Efforts ◦ Seminars/presentations ◦ Introductions ◦ Articles ◦ Cold calls									X	X		
Deliver Your Projects ◦ Proposals ◦ Presentations ◦ Audits											X	

Figure 6.1   Your Couch-to-Corporation Blueprint.

7

Being a
Corporate Therapist

You can consider yourself a corporate therapist when you have your first paying corporate client; you have received a retainer for some portion of your fees and you have a list of deliverables and an agreed upon schedule for meeting them.

Hopefully, you will not experience the same regression that I did when I received my first six figure retainer check. I offer the following anecdote to illustrate the "PAR" nature of performing the corporate therapist role.

The year was 1985 and CDM was six months old. My start-up capital was limited to a modest credit line, a second mortgage on my house, and some cash savings I had borrowed from our joint marital account. As a result, cash flow was a constant worry.

At that time, I had an office, a secretary, and two consultants on staff. Obviously, my first obligation was to keep my organization afloat. I had three corporate clients with billings estimated at approximately $350,000 for the year.

The largest of my CEO clients was a division of a Fortune 100 organization in which a division CEO was a friend of a colleague of mine. As such, I did not apply stringent criteria in qualifying his ability to hire us. The first payment of $25,000 came on time. The second payment, however, did not arrive on time.

The CEO stopped by my office to tell me that he had a problem getting "corporate" to sign off, but the check would be coming within

30 days. I was concerned about the strain this put on cash flow as fees covered the payroll for my staff. However, I dipped into my reserves and waited.

Sixty days came and went. CDM continued to provide services to the CEO's group, as I expected to be paid. However, my concern was turning into panic. To make matters worse, the CEO went on holiday for two weeks.

In the interim, I attempted to borrow more money from a bank. Even with excellent credit, I was turned down. The business was too new to show a track record. So each day, I eagerly checked the mail. No check appeared.

Finally, almost 90 days past due, the CEO phoned me with the news. His corporate boss refused to sign off on our contract. All this time the CEO had been cajoling him into paying us. "But, how could you not have told me?" I asked incredulously. "Maybe, I could have done something! At least we would have stopped the program for non-payment!" "Well," the CEO sighed. "I didn't want to let you down. Besides, it would have made me look awful to can the project midway."

Needless to say, this experience taught me some extremely valuable lessons:

- Never work without a significant retainer upfront.

- Never work if fees are late.

- Never work with friends of friends.

- Most importantly, never be strapped for cash

But these insights came later. At the moment I was more in debt than I had ever been in my life. To make matters worse, I was also in the process of a divorce. Of course, I could have gone to one of my mentors for a loan but I was too proud for that. Instead, I flew to Florida to visit Jennifer Button Tallow (who in spite of this ordeal later came to work as CDM's chief operating officer). Together, we sat on the beach and schemed how I might come into a windfall of money.

I returned from Florida rested if not richer. Awaiting me was a phone call from one of my other CEO clients, who had a lead for me. When I got to his office, he explained he had met William R. on a weekend ski trip, and "Bill" had just been recruited to mastermind the turnaround of a Fortune 100 organization located outside Philadelphia. He told him excitedly about the culture change program he was doing with CDM. William wanted to meet me as soon as possible!

I phoned William's secretary and set up a lunch. To be honest, my confidence was at an all time low. Debt did not become me. However, the lunch meeting was clearly a gift from the gods. William was quite sophisticated in his thinking about people and change. He liked our approach. He felt secure having received such an enthusiastic endorsement from my client. And to my amazement, he hired us on the spot. With lightening speed, he calculated the number of mandays required for the scope of work that I had proposed. The dialogue that unfolded went something like this:

WILLIAM: So, you figure it will take five staff full-time plus yourself, one day a week. Is that right?

IM: Yes, I think so . . . (nervously).

WILLIAM: And you say that your hourly rate is $75, which comes out to be $600 per day. Is that right?

IM: Yes, I believe so . . . (more nervously).

WILLIAM: Well, I just can't pay you that. (abruptly)

IM: Well, I'm sure I could lower the fees given the volume of work . . . (a note of desperation creeping into my voice.)

WILLIAM: No, what I mean is, I can't pay less than $100 an hour to you, or I will look like I hired novices. You don't want that, do you? Christ, I just paid twenty grand to have breakfast with Tom Peters!

IM: Oh. (what else to say?)

WILLIAM: I'll tell you what. I'll pay you $1000 per day and your staff $800 per day. We'll estimate the mandays, at I don't know, 40 weeks?

IM: Okay (mystified).

WILLIAM: I guess you'll want half upfront. So let me go get Rose to cut you a check for $400,000. How's that?

IM: I'm sorry. What did you say? (shock setting in).

WILLIAM: That will cover you for five months and we can get started on the analysis right away. Is that right?

IM: Excuse me. I can take this check today?

WILLIAM: As long as it's before 3 PM. So let me get Rose in here right now. Rosie! (bellowing). Get a check cut for Ms. Martin here!

The trip down the elevator was certainly more surreal than the trip up. As I left, Rose handed me an envelope. William shook my hand vigorously as the elevator doors parted. I smiled weakly and went on my way.

Once inside the safe confines of my car, I began to tremble. The PAR was setting in. As this series of events was too much for me to comprehend, I decided to take the afternoon off. While some might have found the closest bar, I headed straight for the movies.

It was a cold blustery day and I parked as close to the cinema as possible. To this day, I have little memory of the film that I saw. It was, however, of great comfort to sit in the dark and collect myself amid the smell of buttered popcorn.

Upon returning to my car, I eagerly reached into my purse to see the envelope once again. As I scoured around, a wave of panic overtook me. I dumped the contents of my bag onto the passenger seat and frantically combed through them. The check was gone! Or had it ever been real? Could I have imagined it?

As I sat in my car trembling, I replayed my moves since leaving William's office. My heart sank when I realized that I would have to notify Rose immediately to stop payment on the check. Either that or work for free for five months. At that moment, it was hard to tell which was a worse alternative.

As I lumbered out of my car, I noticed a colorful paper corner jutting out from a puddle underneath my car. I reached down, holding my breath. In my hand was the envelope, now soaked, with the logo of William's company. It folded itself limply around my hand. It must have fallen out of my bag when I got out of the car (or at least that is the simplest explanation).

I raced home and retrieved my electric hairdryer. I developed an on the spot procedure for alternately blowing on then ironing the check. Miraculously, it was more or less intact. Certainly it was official-looking enough to present for deposit, although slightly wrinkled. However, the real moral of this story is not about the money.

Being a corporate therapist is an extremely powerful role. The implications of mentoring a chief executive are huge. If you are successful, you will have profoundly helped your client as well as had an enormous impact on his organization. If you fail, you could seriously damage his career and organization.

Your own growth requirements will dictate how much you can take on and how much success you can realistically tolerate. As there will be ongoing regressions, it is important that you make a total commitment to managing your own growth. This may require that you go to therapy to examine how you feel about your new role. At the very least, it will demand that you receive regular weekly clinical supervision.

Being a corporate therapist also requires a different level of legal and financial protection, as the billings and stakes can be quite high. As you assume your new identity, your four best advisors will be your attorney, accountant, money manager, and clinical supervisor. It is worth looking at the role each can play in supporting your new career.

LEGAL IMPLICATIONS

As a corporate therapist, you must present yourself formally to the business community. If you currently have a corporation for your private practice, I recommend that you not involve it in any way in your new endeavor. It is far better to set up a second corporation, preferably a subchapter S. Its name should not have language associated with the practice of psychotherapy. I also recommend that you do not name your new entity after yourself.

While it may be initially ego-gratifying, you may never escape the resentment clients may feel in being assigned to your staff instead of you. Name your entity in a way that is in sync with the services that you expect to offer. And keep some distance between your new corporation and your private practice entity.

In selecting an attorney, negotiate an overall annual retainer paid monthly, rather than an hourly rate. You will need contracts written and reviewed, materials copywritten, deals negotiated, and papers drawn up. A close advisory relationship with a smart lawyer is essential. However, without an agreement upfront, your legal fees can quickly run into the thousands.

Make sure that your lawyer reviews your marketing and presentation materials from a liability perspective. At CDM, each client signs an indemnification contract as well as an agreement that details and limits confidentiality. Your protection against future litigation starts with a careful analysis of how you present yourself and your intentions upfront.

In the event of a lawsuit in which for example, you are accused of practicing psychotherapy under a different representation, the court will evaluate your defense starting with how you've set up your business and defined your services at the outset.

BUSINESS IMPLICATIONS

As a corporate therapist with a growing practice, remember that the IRS agent whom you are destined to meet is your friend. His job is to ensure that your partnership with Uncle Sam is robust and healthy. Knowing this, it behooves you to retain a small business accountant who is familiar with the tax implications of your new business.

Having been audited twice and come through with flying colors, I can tell you firsthand that obeying the IRS rules and keeping excellent records is a must in the consulting industry. There are several considerations in setting up your books:

- You may find that you travel considerably for business. This means you will need an expense form (IRS approved) in which you can delineate and document your travel expenses. (See Figure 7.1.)

- You will be entertaining as well. It is a good idea to have a credit card (like an American Express corporate card) that you can devote to your new entity. This will make monthly reconciliations simple.

- You will need several telephone passwords so that you can track long distance phone and fax charges for various client accounts. You will need a phone credit card to do this.

Be sure to follow the IRS rules for keeping your corporate minutes book. It is the first verification that your corporation is managed as a business instead of an extension of you.

Have your accountant brief you on what to expect from an IRS audit, and set up your files and records correctly now. This way you will be in accordance with the IRS specifications long before an actual audit takes place. This will save months of needless administration later on.

Typically, rapidly increasing revenue triggers an audit. When your income reaches the mid six figures, you enter the realm of the frequently audited. So it pays to be meticulous upfront.

CDM BUSINESS TRAVEL AND RELATED EXPENSES REPORT

| NAME (PLEASE PRINT) | SOCIAL SECURITY NUMBER | PERIOD |
| | | FROM _____ TO _____ |

SUMMARY

COMPANY PAID TRANSPORTATION
All air and rail fares paid by Company should be recorded in this section. Do not add as part of total expenses. The ticket carbon must accompany this report.

MEALS/ENTERTAINMENT
Must be segregated for IRS purposes. Meal cost should not include related tip.

RECEIPTS REQUIRED
The IRS requires all receipts for all lodging, transportation (except local), or any item of $25 or more.

GENERAL
After completion, sign all pages and forward to appropriate manager for approval. Improperly prepared reports will be returned to the approver for amendment.

SOURCE OF CASH ADVANCE IF NOT YOUR OWN

NAME_____

SOCIAL SECURITY NUMBER _____

ADVANCES (DATES OR CHECK NUMBER)

	$
	$
	$

PURPOSE OF TRAVEL/BUSINESS MEAL/ENTERTAINMENT
EXPLAIN TRIPS BUSINESS PURPOSE EVEN WHEN NO BUSINESS MEALS/ENTERTAINMENT EXPENSE ARE INCLUDED

DATE	AMOUNT	BUSINESS PURPOSE AND SUBJECT OF DISCUSSION	NAME, TITLE, AND AFFILIATION OF PERSON DINED (NAME OF ESTABLISHMENT FOR BUSINESS MEALS)

TOTAL ADVANCES RECEIVED $

1. Non Meal/Non Entertainment Expenses (Subtotal A from other side) $
2. Company Car Expenses $
3. Total Non Meal/Non Entertainment Expenses $
4. Total Meal/Entertainment Expenses (Subtotal B from other side) $
5. Total Reimbursable Expenses (Line 3 & Line 4) $
6. Less Total Advances Received (Form Above) $

Balance Due:

☐ Company   ☐ Employee $

Traveler's Signature _____ Date _____

APPROVAL
I HAVE REVIEWED THESE EXPENSES FOR PROPRIETY AND CONFORMANCE TO COMPANY POLICY.

Manager's Signature _____ Date _____

DID YOU REMEMBER ALL RECEIPTS? APPROVAL?

Figure 7.1   CDM Business Travel and Related Expense Report.

(Continued)

The form is rotated 90°. Reading it in its printed orientation:

1	2	3	4	5	6	7	8	9	10	11
DATE	TRAVEL	TRAVELER PAID TRANSPORTATION AMOUNT *	LODGING AMOUNT	PHONE, TOLLS PARKING AMOUNT	OTHER AMOUNT	EXPLANATION OF OTHER	BREAKFAST AMOUNT	LUNCH AMOUNT	DINNER AMOUNT	BUSINESS MEAL & ENTERTAINMENT AMOUNT **
TOTALS						TOTALS				

A. TOTAL NON MEAL/NON ENTERTAINMENT EXPENSES (COL. 3-6)

B. TOTAL MEAL/ENTERTAINMENT EXPENSES (COL. 8-11)

DATE	MANDAYS		CLIENT
	ACTUAL HRS.	BILLABLE HRS.	

*TRANSPORTATION CODE
A - AIR
B - BUS
L - LIMOUSINE
PC - PERSONAL CAR
R - RAIL
T - TAXI
X - RENTAL

**BUS MEAL/ENTERTAINMENT CODE
B - BREAKFAST
L - LUNCH
D - DINNER
O - OTHER

Figure 7.1 Continued

64

As you will be reconciling your records on a month-end basis and summarizing them quarterly and annually, it is useful to negotiate an annual retainer with your accountant as well.

FINANCIAL IMPLICATIONS

Another key advisor is a money manager whose job is to assist you in setting up a portfolio where your financial and retirement goals can be realized. This kind of professional is not simply a stockbroker. A desirable money manager is your financial mentor and conscience. He can help you to become free of financial worries in the future.

Consulting to corporations is lucrative. Fees can range from $1500 to over $10,000 a day. Profit on projects begins at twenty percent of revenues. Once you get your consulting practice off the ground, you will need a structured approach for managing money; both yours and your corporation's. Particularly, if you anticipate collecting retainers upfront, you'll need a strategy for safely investing this money.

I was referred to my money manager by one of my mentors. Having come from modest means, a concept like "interest income" was a revelation to me. My advisor helped me create a financial plan. High on my list was the need for financial security. You, too, will be forced to clarify the role of money in your life and plan accordingly. This will force you to closely examine your values and priorities.

I mention this because the transformation from psychotherapist to corporate therapist can catapult you into a limitless earning capacity where you are no longer bound by the hourly rate that you charged.

PROFESSIONAL IMPLICATIONS

There are many boundary and ethical issues that you must face while practicing in the corporate context. Most can be resolved with careful analysis and deliberate proaction. However, without a clinical supervisor to guide and support you, you will not maintain the clarity of thought needed to prevent yourself from falling into landmines. Consider the following dilemmas:

- ○ The CEO who retained you has asked you to mentor his finance director. In the third session of working together, the finance director tells you he has found a new position and will be terminating his employment. He assumes this information will be held in confidence from the CEO. What do you do?

○ You learn that a disgruntled employee is planning to leak derogatory information about the CEO to a disenchanted board director. The mentee who reveals this is having a problem with this employee and believes his job will be affected if the word gets out. What do you tell him?

○ As you are walking home one evening, you come upon a mentee of one of your staff mentors, engaged in a romantic interlude with a colleague who is clearly not his wife. He sees that you recognize him. Do you tell his mentor or confront him directly? Do you say nothing and leave well enough alone?

○ The CEO's wife has agreed to participate in the mentoring of her husband. In a private session, she confesses that she is having an affair. She begs you to honor this secret. What will you do?

There is, in fact, a right answer in each of these instances, depending upon your view of your role and the rules and boundaries of your corporate therapy practice. As dealing with a system rather than just an individual is so complex; and the authorizer who pays you has certain rights; it is imperative that you clarify your position upfront.

Each of the above examples are true dilemmas that CDM has experienced. In each case, our ability to communicate ground rules upfront led to actions that were acceptable by the parties involved. Here are our responses:

1. The finance director forfeited his right to confidentiality when he disclosed his career plans. The contract of confidentiality clearly states that plans to leave the organization will be reported to the chief executive (who is the legal project authorizer).

2. In the case of the attempted leak to the board, this comes under the Contract as "immoral, illegal, and unethical behavior" and therefore is excluded from the protection of confidentiality. The mentor role-played with the informant mentee how to communicate to the employee that her attempts to thwart the CEO would be stopped.

3. In the case of the lovebirds, the mentor confronted the executive mentee directly, while assuring him he would not reveal what he witnessed to the executive's mentor. He interpreted the dynamics, predicted the imminent disaster to his marriage, and urged the executive to seek help outside the corporation.

4. The CEO's wife was told upfront that events that may affect the CEO's performance at work would be reported to him and were excluded from the confidentiality contract. As she had signed this document, she agreed to eventually discuss the affair, and she and the corporate therapist revealed the affair to the CEO together. While this could have played out in any number of dramas, in this case, the affair was terminated.

Being a corporate therapist is quite an undertaking, albeit with substantial rewards. Coping with your own accelerated growth is extremely challenging. However, look on the bright side. You will certainly be in a position to deeply empathize with the PAR that your corporate clients are experiencing!

In a later chapter, I will discuss another strategy for taking optimal care of yourself during and after your transformation. However, now let's get down to the most difficult task that you face: developing your skills and confidence in marketing and selling your services.

8

Marketing and Selling Corporate Therapy Services

When I joined the management consulting industry, I was most fascinated by the salespeople. They had the impossible job of selling an intangible service that requires a leap of faith to engage in it. Salespeople were also generously compensated in the industry. As a struggling student who had waitressed to finance my education, I was eager to increase my earning potential.

When I tried to learn techniques from the salespeople, however, I found they had little interest in divulging the trade secrets of selling large consulting contracts. In fact, they went to great lengths to prevent me from observing how they converted a reluctant, resistant prospect into a billable client. Having exhausted my arsenal of tactics (which included offering free proposal-writing services and on-the-spot diagnostic profiles) I appealed to David, my mentor at URC. I was then assigned to assist one of URC's most successful and generous-spirited salespeople, Ray Dafrico.

Ray was a former IBM executive. He had tremendous credibility among the senior executives whom he approached with great confidence. The first thing I learned from Ray was to completely research the business of a prospective client as a way of preparing for meetings. Ray maintained extremely high standards for preparation, as "knowledge is power." As a result, his proposals were targeted and taken quite seriously.

Ray believed that the client was always the best teacher, and he performed a valuable mirroring exercise through his ability to listen. He was also frank when discussing a contract. He clearly identified a client's expectations, and based upon them, detailed the proposal. He carefully outlined the approach including services, fees, payment terms, and criteria for measuring results. Nothing was left to conjecture or fantasy. This created high trust within the client who authorized the project.

Under Ray's tutelage, I learned how to sell consultancy services on a large scale. Typical projects were those with budgets starting at one million dollars. As I became skilled on the business side of the sales process, I discovered my psychotherapeutic training to be my ultimate competitive advantage. There are no better sales skills than the ability to bond, listen, and empathize with a potential client. Further, psychotherapeutic training is essential in establishing the climate for positive transference. A prospective client who feels understood will be very receptive to a proposal that adds real value to his business.

Having taught CDM seminars on "Deepening Client Relationships" to diverse groups of professionals including attorneys, accountants, engineers, and physicians, I know firsthand that the idea of selling and promoting one's service is viewed as repugnant. However as a fledgling corporate therapist, consider the following:

1. Throughout your private practice you have proven yourself to be a skillful salesperson. You were just unaware that the skills you used to attract and keep clients were classic selling skills.
2. Having worked in private practice, you are already familiar with a number of the principles of strategic marketing. These include envisioning revenue goals and identifying target markets. It is a natural progression then to identify sources who can help you meet prospective clients as you move from couch to corporation.
3. You must utilize your extensive interpersonal skills in corporate America, just as you did in the privacy of your office. Most importantly, you must now consciously create the architecture of your sales process so that it has a predictable beginning, middle, and end.
4. You must also accept that you may not achieve a fantastic batting average in selling consulting services overnight. At times, I have had a sales conversion rate of 80 percent of qualified

contacts. At other times, I have been unable to generate even a single contract. My process doesn't change and that helps to ensure my confidence in delivering it. However, none of us can sell all of the time.

Once you have envisioned, designed, and documented your marketing and sales process, it will become second nature and at times, effortless and enjoyable. Your natural ability to relate to people will serve you very well.

However, you need to start this journey at the beginning. It requires considerable soul searching to clearly envision your corporate therapy career in a way that is optimal for you. Take the time to complete these next steps alone and with your significant others. They will be invaluable later on. In fact, I feel so strongly about including your spouse or significant other in your new career vision, spouses come free to our seminars.

YOUR CORPORATE THERAPY VISION: WHERE TO START

As I've discussed in the previous chapter, your offering to the corporate marketplace must be based upon your career vision and clinical strengths. Your career vision is your five-year plan which outlines (in writing) how you want to spend your time, your financial and retirement goals, and the work that you love to do. Your vision should be constructed after extensive interviews with your family and an analysis of your successes.

Studying your successes is a crucial step in preparing yourself for transformation. It will also give you permission to envision your ideal career. At CDM, we encourage each staff member to undergo the "Success Interview" with his or her spouse. This exercise includes a chronological review of historical successes, starting with the earliest childhood memory, and working forward through the life cycle. The age frames that we use to delineate life stages are:

0–3 years

3–5 years

5–8 years

8–12 years

12–17 years

17–22 years

22–27 years

28–35 years

35–40 years

40–45 years

45–50 years

50–60 years

60–70 years

In each age frame, ask yourself to recall what experiences made you feel successful, powerful, and competent. Articulate the experience and accompanying feelings to the significant other interviewer. The interviewer's job is to ask questions that will deepen your recall. There are two strategies for doing this.

To help you "go deeper" the interviewer asks: "How did you feel being the captain of the soccer team?" This will assist your recall of feelings associated with success. To help you to "go higher" they ask: "How do you utilize that success today?" This helps you connect the memory to your current skill set. At no time does the interviewer interrupt you, interpret the data, or allow you to drift into negativity. When you recall a disappointment or failure, it is the interviewer's job to politely refocus you back on success. Overall, these strategies help you integrate your successes into your current conscious image of yourself.

When we do this exercise in Corporate Therapy workshops and CDM inductions, psychotherapists initially scoff at the potential value of such a process. However, after the experience, they marvel at how powerful it is to focus exclusively on success. They are also better positioned to examine their clinical strengths.

After completing your success interview, review the patterns that have emerged. You may find that you exhibited leadership at a young age; or that you have always been someone others instinctively trust. Next, examine how you currently utilize these core strengths today. Note any unfulfilled longings. Your career vision should incorporate both core strengths and unmet desires.

Next, examine your successes as a psychotherapist. Pay particular note to those cases in which you felt you might fail. Recall the positive impact that you had on the lives of these clients. Imagine what might have happened without your intervention. Also recall times in which you were inspirational, convincing, and impactful. Recall the feelings that were present when you demonstrated the courage of your clinical convictions. Now, see yourself in the role of corporate therapist, having the same positive impact. You might find yourself in the privacy of an executive's office. You might envision yourself giving a seminar or speech.

Finally, let yourself imagine that if you could earn limitless money, what that would mean to you. How you might live and what you might do. Possessions that you long to acquire and charitable causes you would support. Recognize underlying beliefs and any conflicts that you have regarding money and wealth. Do you feel worthy? Do you feel uncomfortable? What feels right to you regarding your financial goals? How about your retirement? How much money will you need to give you the freedom to pursue non-work related goals? How many years will it take (and at what income level) to achieve these?

After these inner journeys, you are ready to construct your corporate therapy vision. Write your mission statement, approach to the marketplace, basic positioning and expectations for revenue. For example:

> It is my mission to provide a mentoring service to executives in my local community. I expect to generate between $250,000 and $500,000 per year in contracts and workshop fees. I expect my business to grow 20 percent per year and to include associates. I will market myself through brown bag lunch presentations to executive groups. I expect to generate three corporate contracts and four workshops in year one.

Once you have defined your overall vision, you can fill in the missing details. How much time will you allow for the transition? How many days per week can you devote to your new career? How much money do you need to justify a career change? How will you fund your start-up? How will you manage your time? Who can best support and discipline you to stay on target?

YOUR CORPORATE THERAPY OFFERING

Considerable deliberation is required to arrive at a cohesive and integrated offering of products and services. While your offering is based upon your strengths, it is dangerous to be too eclectic. The marketplace will "position" you at a result of your packaging of yourself. You must take care not to confuse them regarding your intentions and services.

Therefore, you need to arrive at a one or two sentence positioning statement that explains your offering. While CDM's positioning is quite broad ("culture transformation to improve competitive advantage" or "leadership transformation through accelerated growth"), yours can be more narrow. You might say, "executive coaching to improve business performance," or "customer analysis to expand marketshare," or "facilitation to enhance teamwork." Whatever positioning statement you choose must meet the following criteria:

- It must be short; no more than two sentences;

- It must convey your offering and its benefits;

- It must be easy to understand and remember;

- It must be consistent with your vision and strengths.

To define yourself as an "organization consultant" or even a "corporate therapist" is not enough to position you in the marketplace. Corporate clients will want to know your focus and how it will benefit them. Further, they need to know which budget will cover your services. While there is typically an overall "management services" budget for consultants, there are also categories such as "executive development," "management education," and "research." The easier you make it to pigeonhole you through a positioning statement, the better.

Be careful not to attempt too broad an offering. For example, if you specialize in women's issues and teambuilding, the marketplace will assume that you work with teams of women. In my own case, I had to abandon a series of seminars that I offered to women in the mid-1980s ("Women and Intimacy"). While they were popular, lucrative, and well promoted on television, my CEO clients complained they were being teased by their colleagues that they had retained "that intimacy lady." My positioning had gotten confused.

PACKAGING YOURSELF

Once you have defined your offering, you must name your new entity and develop your packaging. While this is a creative endeavor, if you are not artistically inclined, it can be frustrating.

An excellent source of talent for this task can be found in the graduate departments of art schools or universities. Place an ad in the university newspapers that you are seeking proposals and samples of creative work for a logo and package design. I still find graduate students are far more innovative than most professionals, as their creativity is not yet harnessed. If you seek a more experienced eye, the creative staff of major ad agencies also moonlight. You will receive award-winning packaging at a fraction of the cost. They can also prepare camera ready artwork and mechanicals for printing.

Before you commit to printing your materials, show your final concepts to corporate friends or business associates. Gauge their reactions to your package. Is it clear, inviting, captivating, and upbeat? Does it encourage them to meet with you? What does it say about you and your service? When we at CDM develop a new product, we take as long as six months to select a final image based upon client reactions.

When you are comfortable that your package promotes your service in the best possible light, bid out your printing to get the best price. Remember that you will need a reliable printer in the future. You will need business cards (your name, title, address, phone, fax, tag line, and logo), letterhead and envelopes, stickers for mailing, presentation covers (a 8″ × 11″ folder with your logo), notepads, and a simple brochure. It is best to write your own copy and have a copywriter edit it. Figure 8.1 illustrates a simple brochure that CDM has used effectively for ten years.

You must also devote attention to packaging your image, as it is the only tangible proof of your service besides your brochure! Take a hard look at yourself, then compare what you see to what business executives symbolize in general. Corporate clients expect consultants to look like themselves. Deviations from the norm, including facial hair, trendy clothes, pipes, hats, and tweed blazers are not easily accepted. Simple tailored clothing in blue, gray, or black, a wool coat or trench coat, and expensive accessories (shoes, briefcase, and handbag) are the norm. We at CDM joke about maintaining a wardrobe of "corporate regalia" reserved for on-site visits or presentation days. Designers such as Armani, Ralph Lauren, Donna Karan, and Anne Klein best sum up the classic elegant corporate look. I mention this because I have spent considerable time defending staff member's images to CDM clients, as well as tactfully mentioning essential changes in image.

The psychology of this is rather simple. If an executive has invited you on-site, he has brought you home to meet the family. He does not want to be embarrassed that you "don't fit in" with his elk.

Short of Transformation, It Just Can't Happen

○ Achieving breakthroughs in sales, quality, morale, productivity and profitability requires transformation.
○ Merging two organizations in a way which ensures there is one vision and culture requires transformation.
○ Keeping pace with the CEO's vision and expectations requires transformation.
○ Shaping the marketplace and transcending the competition requires transformation.
○ Readying an organization to lead an industry requires transformation.

Only transformation ensures that organizations can outgrow old, familiar, safe routines that limit success and inhibit quantum leaps in performance.

CDM provides the context, process, expertise and support to implement a four-phase corporate transformation process that is easy to monitor and measure bottom-line results. Utilizing a mentoring systems model, CDM assists CEOs and senior executives in creating the culture for outstanding, ongoing self-sustaining success.

As a result of transformation:

○ Leaders become mentors.
○ Managers and supervisors become leaders.
○ Employees live for the weekly numbers.
○ Customers become sponsors, avid fans and referral sources.
○ Products and services become a new way of life for customers.
○ Support areas and operations are structured for zero error service.
○ There is one integrated culture aligned to deliver daily results.

Corporate transformation means making it happen instead of just talking about it or dabbling in it. Call us to schedule a presentation of our corporate success stories: Creative Dimensions In Management, Inc., Lee Park, Main Building, Suite 200, 1100 East Hector Street, Conshohocken, PA 19428, (610) 825-8350.

Figure 8.1   Brochure Featuring the Corporate Transformation Process.

TARGETING YOUR MARKET

Your next challenge is to identify potential clients for your service. You need to consider both industry and geographic factors. Does your service lend itself to a particular industry in a timely way (e.g., stress management workshops for attorneys), or can your offering be generalized across several industries (e.g., the coaching of business executives)? Is there a particular industry that appeals to you? Do you want to specialize, therefore build your reputation within a specific market?

There are advantages and disadvantages to industry specialization. You will develop your reputation as a consultant within a particular framework and referrals will come easily. However, if you become too closely identified with the industry, it will be difficult to expand later on. Benefits include taking advantage of the learning curve, building credibility quickly, and establishing a contact base. It is up to you based upon what ideally supports your vision.

Another key consideration is geography. How far are you willing to travel for work? Having become both a local Marcus Welby and a global citizen, I can tell you firsthand that both approaches work equally well. If you dislike overnight travel, then focus on organizations within 100 miles of your office or home. If you are free to be away from home, you can pursue leads anywhere that strikes your fancy. While initially exciting, traveling takes its toll on your energy level, overall health, and intimate relationships. However, corporate consulting is an opportunity to literally see the world.

In my case, my penchant for global shopping motivated me to take assignments in countries that have crafts that I collect. I was able to examine art, furniture, crafts, and food preparation in addition to conducting interesting work. There are many international consultants as well who combine their personal and business interests. They combine assignments with safaris, ski trips, family holidays, and hobby shows. With current frequent flyer programs, there is certainly an incentive to travel. You can collect air miles that can be applied to free fabulous holidays.

Once you have determined the industries and geographies in which you will market yourself, it is time to generate your prospect list. While this research takes time and effort, today's computer services makes it easier than ever before.

You can find lists of targeted organizations on the Internet or in your local library. *Forbes, Fortune,* and *Inc.* publish various lists annually.

Your business library keeps directories of all local businesses, industry associations, and chambers of commerce. Further, there is software available that details business organizations by state and industry.

Many reference materials also detail personnel, including Board members and key executives. Utilizing these, you need to build a list of 100 targeted prospects. Next, color code them by how likely it is that you will be able to meet with an authorizer of consulting services.

APPROACHING YOUR TARGET MARKET

In our corporate therapy workshops, psychotherapists are amazed by how many people they already know who can help secure sales meetings. Neighbors, classmates, friends, and colleagues can assist you in getting first meeting appointments. It is only your current and past therapy patients who are off-limits to approach for help.

The best kind of first meeting is through an endorsement or referral. It creates a better foundation for building a client relationship. I have detailed in Chapter 6 how to utilize power brokers in arranging introductions for a fee in the event that your network is limited.

As I've mentioned, be sure to qualify prospects prior to setting up an appointment. Generally, only CEOs and their direct reports authorize consultancy services. These executives include directors of marketing, manufacturing, sales, operations, strategic planning and human resources, information technology, engineering, and quality.

Your first meeting with a prospective client is the most important. Therefore, preparation is crucial. Learn as much as possible about the client's future vision, current challenges, key successes, organization structure, and past performance. Write out narratives and rehearse them before the call. Role-play with your significant other how you would like the call to unfold. Especially, write a meeting agenda that you can refer to privately during the meeting.

Going to meetings without an agenda is a fireable offense within CDM. It is a flagrant waste of time and energy for the consultant not to set goals and expectations upfront. An agenda typically includes the following:

1. Results of a very successful meeting.
2. Objectives of the meeting.
3. Anticipated barriers.

4. Process steps and sequence of events.
5. Precise narratives.

You can also review it after the meeting to critique your performance.

SELLING YOUR SERVICES: A SIMPLE SALES PROCESS TO MASTER

Selling a consulting service should take no more than five meetings and can take as few as two. Keep in mind the greater the number of meetings, the less likely it is that there will be a signed contract. This is true of sales processes in general. If you are meeting with an authorized decision maker, the process is efficient. If indecision lags on, the prospect is too conflicted or ambivalent to buy your service.

Expect initially to sell one-tenth of prospective clients with whom you meet. This will help you plan your face-to-face customer contact time. Over time, your sales rate will improve. A four out of five rate is considered excellent among top salespersons.

The following section outlines an effective process for selling consulting services. Once you have customized it to meet your needs and objectives, do not change it! You will only be able to evaluate your skills in selling corporate therapy services by presenting your service in a consistent manner.

Meeting Number One: Bonding and Exploration of Possibilities/Opportunities

Your first meeting with a prospective client should build a positive, trusting relationship. The best strategy for accomplishing this is to listen. Active listening promotes bonding and the projection needed for transference as well as ensures your understanding of his dilemma.

Start by commending the prospective client on past and current successes that his organization has achieved. Interview him about his career history and current role. Ask him questions about the organization's vision, immediate challenges, and annual goals. Done correctly, this interview should take approximately 30 minutes.

When your prospect asks you to describe yourself and your services, tailor your answer to his organization's current needs. Discuss whether his organization uses consultants such as yourself. He may ask you to suggest a "next step" for proposing initial work. Be aware: This is a buying signal.

After outlining a few scenarios, ask if it is appropriate to write a proposal that you and your prospect can review at a later date. This is your first test closing. If his answer is no, it is time to move on.

If his answer is yes, find out what expectations he has for a consulting proposal. Is there a particular format he prefers? What elements can be included to expedite his decision-making process? Who else will be reading it?

This collaborative effort will deepen your initial bond with this prospective client. It will further serve you in not wasting time preparing a document that is incomplete or unacceptable. Also set a date before you leave for your next appointment. Agree to review the proposal together and evaluate its merits and the benefits of a joint project.

When you arrive at your office, compose and fax a brief note within 24 hours of the meeting. For example:

Dear George:

I really enjoyed meeting you and I look forward to our work session on the 22nd. I appreciate your time and interest in my work. In thinking about our discussion, I will give considerable thought in how to assist you in strengthening the leadership of your core team.

Thanks again and take care.

Business writing should be warm and stark. It can also be an excellent medium for building a nurturant client relationship. Make it your habit to regularly send cards, notes, and small work-related gifts. Your relationship with your client is the first place that you demonstrate added value as a corporate therapist.

In preparation for your second meeting, you will also need to write a proposal. Consulting proposals are typically brief and a long document will not be appreciated. Two or three pages is adequate. The proposal typically contains the following sections:

- Cover letter.

- Description or justification for the project.

- ○ Scope of work.

- ○ Financial implications or cost.

- ○ Schedule of key activities and events.

- ○ Next steps.

Edit your proposal so that it is clear, concise, and easy to accept. From a neurolinguistic programming perspective, it should strategically create a yes set in your prospective client's mind.

Do not mail or fax the proposal prior to the second appointment. It will not facilitate the sale, no matter what the prospect says. You owe it to yourself to present your proposals in person.

Meeting Number Two: Proposal Review and Initial Close

The purpose of the second meeting is to continue the relationship-building process with your prospective client. The medium you will use to do this is your proposal. If this is a collaborative effort, it will continue to be during this review meeting.

To continue the bonding process, begin the meeting by focusing on how the prospect is doing and any news he has to report. Do not short circuit this process by rushing into your agenda. I have personally witnessed more sales failures from discounting the client's agenda than from any other error. Remember, being with you should be therapeutic in and of itself!

When the prospective client signals he is ready to focus on your proposal, be proactive and review it at length. This is your opportunity to communicate your vision, enthusiasm, and confidence in the proposed project. If bonding has occurred, this enthusiasm is infectious. In my own experience, clients often tell me they committed to do a CDM program partially on the basis of my conviction.

It is important to state the benefits of your proposed project clearly. Do not expect the prospect to see obvious connections. You need to educate him. For instance, "mentoring will shorten the learning curve for new hires" or "teambuilding creates a very open spirit for debate" are necessary clarifications.

There will be discussion and debate following the presentation of your proposal. You can assess whether the prospect sees the need for

your service. If not, it is time to move on. You can sell someo
the benefits of utilizing your service versus the competitor; however, it
is impossible to convince someone of needing your service. Either
they perceive the need or not. There is no point in preaching to the
unconverted.

The chances are if your prospect has requested a proposal, the
need is understood. If so, this meeting becomes an evaluation of
whether he believes your service will meet this need. This is often an
intuitive decision based upon the bond that has been established to
date. Selling services means "buying" the service provider.

The decision to engage you is often made between the second and
third meeting. Some prospects feel overwhelmed by the idea of beginning a new consulting project with all it entails. Others want to discuss
the proposal with colleagues and staff. To keep the pace and momentum, schedule a third meeting within two weeks of this one. This third
meeting can be done by telephone.

You may find that the prospect requests you to make a presentation
to his team members. This is certainly a next step toward authorizing a
project. However, be clear that you expect your prospect to lead this
decision-making process. Decisions by consensus are not practical or
realistic.

There are times when the sale is closed in the second meeting,
even in the first! However, don't despair if your prospect wants to be
thoughtful. You have other prospective clients to call upon in the
interim.

Meeting Number Three:
The Negotiation and Close

In meeting number three, your prospect becomes a client. He will
agree to the proposal in principle, but will negotiate the scope of work
and your fees. It is important that you support the spirit of negotiation,
as it is a ritual for most corporate executives.

Do not be dismayed when your new client decreases the scope of
work. He is protecting himself against exposure, as you are a new "object" in his world. Executives are conservative, and most consulting
work is generally sold in extensions. When he attacks your fees, however, stand strong! Working for less than you deserve leads to resentment
later on. "Come on, Roger" you might say, "If I save one nonperforming

manager through mentoring him, you will save $75,000 in recruiting fees."

This ritual is generally brief and relatively painless. It ends with a handshake, symbolizing "the deal." It's now time to plan the startup of the project; how to announce it and who it will include. This may occur now or in meeting number four.

Before the next meeting, you will need to detail your agreement in a legal contract, reviewed by your attorney and signed by both parties.

Meeting Number Four: Project Positioning and Startup

There is only one effective way to correctly position a consulting project: that is with a formal corporate announcement. This should be a letter from the client that details the purpose, objectives, expectations, and participants as well as any calendar requirements. Typically, you would draft this announcement and have your client edit and personalize it. It should be brief and clear. For example:

To: Management Team

To assist us in accelerating the achievement of our corporate vision, we have engaged the services of XXXX. This group is a competent supplier of mentoring services for executives. My team and I will initially pilot the program. To kick off this project, we and the planning committee will be confidentially interviewed regarding progress toward our vision.

Please be candid with the consulting team. You will sign a contract of confidentiality prior to your interview. A feedback session regarding the summary of our responses will be held on January 11th at 10 AM in conference room B. Please allow two hours for the meeting. If you have any questions, feel free to contact me at X4763.

I look forward to my own mentoring and I hope that you find this service beneficial. We will formally evaluate it by a confidential audit after six months.

There is nothing more annoying to an organization than having outside consultants stumbling around who have not been formally acknowledged. This step is crucial in both positioning your credibility and symbolizing an endorsement from the senior executive group.

Another startup activity is determining who will participate in your project. Your client will establish the criteria and together you will make the selections. Once you know the target population, draft a letter to them and distribute it individually, detailing the project and your credentials. This package should be reviewed by your client as well. Then schedule your initial interviews.

Now that you are on your way, remember the following do's and don'ts of consulting:

DO'S OF CORPORATE CONSULTING

Do entertain your clients regularly. Lunches, dinners, sports events, and conferences are appropriate social occasions. Bonding must continue to deepen. Unlike private patients, your corporate clients expect to be entertained, and social occasions are excellent update and strategy sessions.

Do give appropriate gifts such as books, CDs, audiotapes, gift baskets, and videos. Make sure that you note birthdays and send cards. This nurturing is not expected and will be much appreciated.

Do document your project weekly as well as any changes in its scope and direction. Start this process by preparing a contract and making sure it is signed before you begin work. All changes in scope require client sign-off as well.

Do detail your payment terms and collect fees prior to delivering work. This starts with a preliminary retainer.

Do give formal presentations of successes and project progress and barriers once or twice a month. The consulting process requires endless justification and salesmanship, as well as client direction and support to keep it effective.

DON'TS OF CORPORATE CONSULTING

Don't ignore the client's support personnel, like secretaries and administrative assistants. They can make or break your project. Include them in gifts and other forms of acknowledgment.

Don't promise what you can't deliver or commit to unrealistic timeframes. Clients detest consultants who oversell their contribution or can't deliver on time.

Don't assume any client knowledge that you learn is in the public domain. Do not discuss your clients with anyone except your clinical supervisor. Many profitable relationships have been destroyed by "airplane socializing."

Don't ask for referrals. Wait until sufficient reciprocity is built and they will come spontaneously. Give your corporate clients time to see the benefits in what you provide.

Don't abuse your client relationship by becoming a broker of sorts. Other consultants will approach you for referrals to your top clients. If you believe their services are needed, then make an introduction. However, taking fees for this reduces you to being a "broker."

FEES AND BILLING

Your fees as a corporate therapist should be commensurate with the industry standard as well as your training and experience. Check to see what consulting services cost in your area. Per hour fees range from $175 to $500 per hour. Per diem fees range from $600 to $5000 or more per day.

Set your fees correctly. Once they are set, they are hard to change. Further, stay away from "incentive deals" in which your fees are a percentage of business results; or stock ownership in exchange for money. Both of these arrangements, while lucrative, require considerable expertise to manage correctly.

The best billing process is 50 percent upfront and 50 percent at midpoint. Billing in thirds typically leads to problems collecting the final payment. Ensure that you receive your retainer upfront. Late payment should be penalized by 5 percent if received after 30 days.

MARKETING YOURSELF

While meeting with a prospective client in his or her office is the goal, you need to continually "fill the pipeline" so that first appointments are forthcoming. There are several approaches to marketing yourself that are effective in getting results from an investment of time and money.

Speeches, Presentations, and Brown Bag Lunches

Public speaking is an excellent way to position and present yourself to qualified prospects. Industry associations, trade shows, and television appearances are effective media for attracting potential clients. It is well worth the effort to research opportunities where you can present. All major industry associations have an annual conference as well as regular get-togethers. You can contact their public relations personnel in order to submit a workshop proposal. For easy acceptance, make your topic provocative and timely. For example, "Succession Planning in the Family Business: Renewal or Betrayal?" was a popular title for CDM when marketing to large family businesses.

"Brown bag lunches" can be an effective entry for making sales presentations within targeted corporations. Write to the Human Resource director and offer to give a free seminar at lunchtime in the conference room for approximately 10 to 15 attendees. You supply the presentation; the corporation supplies a buffet lunch. Typically, attendees are prospects or those who can notify prospects. Your topic should reflect your service without being a sales pitch. For example, "the challenge of accelerating growth" can be an effective presentation topic that naturally leads into the benefits of mentoring.

The brown bag approach is extremely effective in obtaining mentoring contracts with mid-size organizations such as law firms, accountancies, and advertising agencies. It will not, however, be effective in securing large-scale transformation projects. These take an intimate bond with the chief executive authorizer.

Networking

Networking can be an effective method for announcing yourself to the marketplace. However, networking events attract so many competitors that prospects get confused and overwhelmed with the parade of service providers. Networking events can be a useful opportunity if you are sure that a prospect will be attending. You can say a quick hello, offer your package, and agree to phone for a face-to-face appointment. The key is to differentiate yourself by utilizing your relational skills. Humor can be a quite effective tool. I often say, "Well, it is certainly your lucky day to meet a consultant who is a shrink *and* a female! The worst of all evils!" This leads to an acknowledgment of the fantasies most clients have about psychological professionals in our field, and helps break the ice.

Joint Ventures

Joint ventures with other consultancies can be invaluable in assisting you to both broaden your offering and widen your customer base. For examples for CDM, our relationship with IBM was an excellent source of introductions to financial services institutions. We are more recently in a strategic alliance with the Thomas Group International, a public company that specializes in organizational transformation for total business entities through decreasing the cycle times that impact their operating results. TGI's performance is so consistent that it takes a substantial part of its fees in incentives tied to bottomline performance improvement. Its global customer base are Fortune 500 companies. In this venture, CDM will provide culture transformation services to support the rapid improvement in business performance and competitive advantage.

How do you determine which organizations might best compliment your services and broaden your offering? The following are considerations to ponder:

- Your joint-venture partner should have access to different market segments and be willing to provide introductions.

- Your combined offering should enhance your competitive advantage as well as provide an integrated approach. This requires an analysis of both processes in order to design a seamless consulting process.

- Your values, style, and philosophies should be similar in nature, so that teamwork is optimal. You cannot afford internal conflicts that drain energy from your combined client work.

- Your potential partner should have a successful track record, growth rate, and excellent reputation. Certainly, you do not want to hitch your star to a wagon in decline.

Outplacement firms, executive search firms, and operational consultancies are good possibilities to consider. Further, consultants who do similar work but are not direct competitors can be referral sources as well. For example, advertising agencies often subcontract customer analysis work or refer psychologically based research studies.

Advertising

Advertising is typically ineffective in delivering qualified prospects to your door. While it will promote your image and build awareness about your service, the market is overloaded with consulting products and providers. The industry has a reputation for poor delivery as well. Your message, even if well-packaged and presented, may be met with suspicion if you are a newcomer.

If you are offering a seminar, however, advertising can be an excellent medium. You will need to take sufficient space to detail your offering and supply a contact number. Often, prospects sign up over the phone with credit card numbers to confirm their space. The key is to advertise in newspapers that are popular with your target audience. You will need to experiment with many approaches and track your conversion rate in order to determine what works best for you.

Now knowing how to market yourself, we need to examine one more pitfall. How to balance your private practice and your emerging corporate therapy consultancy?

9

Balancing Private Practice and Corporate Therapy

One of the greatest dilemmas psychotherapists who are graduates of our Corporate Therapy Seminars face is: WHEN to make the leap? Resolving when and how to wind down one's private practice in order to pursue corporate therapy work full-time is a tricky task. If you don't devote enough time to building your corporate practice, you will not generate enough work to justify a career transition. Yet, every hour that you devote to transisting into your new career can be spent doing therapy with a current patient who can refer others.

There is, however, a logical approach to engineering your transition. It requires discipline, dedication, sacrifice, and time management. Yet, within a year, you will be able to decide when and if to make the plunge.

You need to start by recognizing that your work week is now seven instead of five or six days. While you have family and social commitments, you will need extra time to pursue various activities that are part of your transition. Unfortunately, most clinicians cannot initially take time away from their current practice. There are, however, many tasks that can be accomplished in the evenings and on weekends. Some of these can be done with your significant others as well.

The self-preparation work outlined in Chapter 7 can be done in your free time. Your business plan can be written in a couple of weekends. Business associates and corporate friends can be interviewed over lunch or dinner. Sporting events can also be a great place to test out your new career plans with trusted mentors or advisors. Developing your offering, positioning, and packaging can also be done in nonbillable hours. Your marketing research and prospect lists can be accomplished during weekends as well.

Attending sales calls is the first commitment you must make that requires you to sacrifice your clinical work. Further, as much as you might like to restrict this activity to the same day each week, it is highly unlikely that your prospect will be amenable or available. Your life quickly becomes a juggling act from the moment you walk onsite to call on your first prospective corporate client. How you manage to cope with the inherent conflicts that emerge in attempting two careers will ultimately determine the success of your transition.

The following strategies have worked well for both CDM staff and CTS graduates.

NOTIFY YOUR PATIENTS UPFRONT

Since you will inevitably have to juggle your therapy appointments to accommodate a last minute change in your corporate therapy schedule, it is helpful to prepare your patients upfront. Those patients with abandonment issues can be negatively impacted when your priorities appear to shift. Our psychotherapist graduates in transition have found alerting their private cases that they have undertaken consulting projects that require travel has established the expectation and permission for flexibility. You may also find, as they have, that patients are basically supportive of such a move given the current realities of the healthcare industry.

ORGANIZE YOUR TIME (ALL OF IT)

You may currently keep an annual schedule of events, in which your monthly and weekly commitments are tracked. However, this transition dictates that you account for every waking and sleeping hour! Lay out your schedule to identify any and all possible free time. This might be early in the morning or late at night. Then, schedule your corporate therapy tasks with deadlines for completion. For example, writing this book while running CDM required that I write in the evening after 10:00 PM. This meant I started my days later in order to accommodate working into the night. I also devoted all travel time to my writing project, whether it was on an airplane or in a car where I could dictate my thoughts. I was also not above writing while traveling uphill on a ski lift!

Once you "manload" your schedule with time allocations for all corporate therapy tasks, it should take about three months to prepare yourself, develop your approach and complete your marketing materials.

PREPARE YOUR FAMILY

The couch to corporation transition is a transformation. As such, it will generate a shift in identity. Your significant others need to be educated as well as "sold" on the benefits of your new vision. They need to support both your regressions and depressions, as well as be willing to give you more private time. Hold a family conference in which you can present the rationale for considering such a direction. Clearly spell out the magnitude of the change and the support that you will require. Appoint a designated disciplinarian to ensure that you stay on schedule.

The role of this disciplinarian is quite useful to you during this time. If you have a spouse or significant other, he or she can be empowered to oversee your transition. If not, a close friend can be called upon for strategic support. The disciplinarian once empowered with permission, is expected to confront you regularly about your progress. If you slack off, the disciplinarian can inspire as well as punish you to get you back on track!

Having been involved with the PAR model of transformation for over a decade, I freely accept my own regressive episodes. To minimize both their frequency and impact, I call a meeting with my husband. Together, we examine my history to uncover any beliefs or experiences that will sabotage my success in the new endeavor. We then predict how and when I might "regress." He also reviews my progress to keep me focused and productive. Not only does he feel equally responsible for actualizing my vision, he is as pleased as I to celebrate when my "next lifetime" has been successfully realized. Obviously, we reverse roles when needed.

GET OUT AND ABOUT

One of the greatest terrors that clinicians face is having to physically leave their offices. But now the world is your office! There is a very real agoraphobia that develops in response to working within one room all day. It may not rear its ugly head until you take the plunge to go out frequently, but tremendous anxiety may build order to keep you confined in "a room of one's own."

Consider this to be a very natural reaction to giving up the control that you feel in your treatment room. In the outside world, you will have to rely on your social skills to sell yourself as a potential corporate therapist. Initially, this may feel quite strange. Again, there is safety in numbers.

When you attend a networking event, take your spouse along. Divide up the room and agree to conquer it together. You can both spend one hour passing out your business cards, then meet at a bar for a progress report. Afterwards you can regress over a romantic dinner with a bottle of your favorite wine.

In time, being "out there" will feel quite enjoyable. In the transition though, you might feel the awkwardness similar to that of being single again.

USE MENTORS

As I've discussed, mentors are an invaluable support system during your transition. Your current clinical supervisor can be the first person that you engage as your ally. The move from private to corporate practice entails a total review and revision of your role, identity, boundaries, ethics, and treatment approach. Your supervisor will both empathize and strategize with you as you actively construct your new role.

A business mentor would be useful as well. If you have a colleague or friend who is in the corporate world, consider engaging him or her as a mentor. This person can help you both understand and infiltrate corporate America. You can attend networking events and conferences. He or she can be the translator as well as guide as you move from your office into the world-at-large office setting.

In my own experience, there is little worth doing without lining up an appropriate mentor. Not only is time saved in learning upfront what would have taken years to experience firsthand, a trusted guide is an inspiration and pathfinder rolled in one.

In contracting with a mentor, it is important to obey the inherent rules of the relationship. Mentors must be available upon demand; willing to be intimate, noncompetitive, and generous-spirited. Your role is to appreciate their time and experiences. Mentoring should be amply rewarded as well. Give your mentor gifts as well as the joy of hearing of your triumphs. When managed correctly, both mentor and mentee grow and benefit from the relationship.

KEEP IT STRAIGHT

One of the greatest challenges that you face is to maintain two separate and distinct identities without feeling "torn in half." As a clinician, you have a persona, reputation, and role in helping others. As a corporate therapist, your self-presentation will be quite different. The disparity between these two roles can be quite dramatic as you change hats during each day or week.

One way to "keep it straight" is to separate your two careers totally. This means separate corporations, bank accounts, offices, and phone lines. At the very least, you can utilize your current office for your clinical work and obtain other space for your corporate practice, even if temporarily it is in your own home.

Attempting to create an umbrella under which your clinical and corporate identities both exist is a mistake. Not only will this strategy fail to convince others that the two roles co-exist, you will feel more pressure than if you delineate the two practices completely.

Against our recommendation, one of our seminar graduates elected to start a center in which he combined his private and corporate practices. Patients and mentees alike could be found in his waiting room or at his seminars. Before long, both groups resented the privileges of the other. He became confused as to what he represented to whom within each context. Eventually, he gave up corporate therapy and returned to private practice full-time.

START SMALL

In order to successfully transist into full-time corporate practice, you must generate enough revenue to replace your private practice income, as well as additional monies to fund your startup (approximately $25,000 in the first year) and overhead (30 percent of ongoing revenue). This requires that you secure at least two consulting contracts before making the leap.

You only need one excellent project under your belt for your corporate therapy practice to naturally grow. However, in order for it to be a phenomenal success, you must stay focused and start small.

Let's say, for example, that your offering is a mentoring service. Over a brown bag lunch, you have interested the senior partners of a law firm sufficiently to get a modest program of ten or so participants started. Stop here! It is not necessary to push for more work until your first six-month audit is completed. Take the time to do your cases with excellence. Get the appropriate supervision. Work on your own growth barriers. Give yourself the space and permission to "straddle" your corporate and private practices. In time, two days a week of mentoring will grow into five days. Your mentees will make sure of it through word of mouth if your work is superior.

It is a huge mistake to underestimate the challenges of your new career. As an employer of clinicians, I can attest to their traumas when they bite off too much too soon. At CDM, we have learned to temper the enthusiasm of fledgling corporate therapists. First assignments rarely entail more than two days a week for up to one year.

INSIST ON RETAINERS

In order to provide yourself with both maximum revenue as well as peace of mind, insist that your corporate therapy services be billed as annual retainers. A mentoring program, for instance, takes at least one year to be effective. If you receive two six-month payments, you can forecast your annual revenue and decrease your therapy practice accordingly. Corporate clients are used to paying retainers.

This approach can work effectively with project work as well. A customer analysis or culture analysis can be billed in two payments — startup and midpoint. Seminars should be billed as one upfront payment based upon either a per diem or cost per attendee. Make sure that you protect yourself by collecting your fees properly. Each dollar that you generate and collect gets you closer to your goal of full-time corporate practice.

TERMINATE WITH CARE

Like most clinicians, you may be feeling the wear and tear of conducting therapy with highly challenging cases. Our graduates have treated everyone from multiple personality disorders to adult incest survivors and severe borderlines. Understandably, they long for the more "normal" world of the corporate client where they can expect to see faster progress and better results. But like yourself, they have made long-term commitments for healing. Disengagement is a complex strategic process.

You may elect to complete all of your therapy cases before you move on. You may decide that many patients can be referred. Whatever approach that you take, factor in termination time in your overall transition plan.

You can reorganize your private practice to seeing patients only in the evenings. You might devote Saturdays to keep up with your clinical obligations. But don't underestimate the energy it will take long-term to optimally complete your therapy cases while delivering superior consulting services as well.

To help you plan your transition, Chapter 10 provides you with an overview of the many corporate consulting processes that you can incorporate into your tool kit. Some are long-term; some are project-oriented. You can pick and choose based upon your vision and current commitments.

PART THREE
Doing Corporate Therapy

10

A Corporate Therapist's Tool Kit

In providing corporate therapy, there are as many approaches as there are to conducting psychotherapy in one's office. Depending upon your vision and clinical strengths, you can focus on either individuals or groups. You can specialize in training and education or focus on intrapsychic processes. You can support several kinds of evolutionary processes as well. You might help executives change companies or careers. Conversely, you might do retirement counseling. If you are an expert in diagnosis, you might gravitate toward executive search screening or culture analysis projects. There is certainly enough opportunity to showcase your talents and skills.

In determining what to put into your tool kit, I have summarized a variety of consulting interventions that can be delivered by a corporate therapist. While many of these are also delivered by change management consultants, a clinical background and perspective is far superior in obtaining optimal results.

CHARACTER ASSESSMENT

You can assist the CEO or senior executive in recruiting and selecting mentally healthy executives. This can be sold directly to the corporate client or subcontracted through an executive search firm.

Typically, the CEO retains an executive search organization to find candidates for various middle and senior-level positions. The search firm receives an average fee of up to 30 percent of the new hire's annual package (salary, bonus, and benefits) to fill the position. The search firm then researches and contacts possible recruits. These are typically found in competitor organizations. The search firm screens and interviews possible candidates. The CEO is then asked to interview a short list.

It is at this time that the skills of the corporate therapist can be invaluable. Poor hiring decisions which are quite common, can literally cost millions. Consider the following actual CDM example.

I was referred to the chairman of a large national savings and loan. He had built the organization for over 30 years. He was in his midsixties and eager to retire. Upon his board's recommendation, he retained a local well-reputed search firm and recruited a high profile New York executive from another industry to be CEO and president. To entice him to give up the glamour of the Big Apple, he agreed to a generous package of base salary (in 1987, $475,000 per annum), bonus (based upon operating results, up to 100 percent of salary), and stock options (estimated worth: $3.2 million). The new CEO came onboard and installed himself in the executive suite. The chairman crossed his fingers and prayed.

After nine months, it was obvious to everyone that something might be wrong with "Dick." The chairman confided to another CDM client that he feared that he had made a serious mistake. Over dinner, he asked me to attend a corporate function to observe Dick. He was concerned that Dick would be offended to be referred to a psychotherapist.

If there ever was a narcissist in motion, it was Dick on the evening of my surveillance. He endlessly bragged about himself. He played piano and sang raucous songs. He drank too much. He ignored key executives and suppliers in favor of those who listened eagerly to his war adventures. He made sexual advances to a young saleswoman whom he enticed to be his piano seatmate. In the wee hours, he tore himself away with an entourage to go clubbing. As they piled into the corporate limo, he was carrying a Scotch and soda in a paper cup.

I had the unfortunate job of breaking the news to the chairman that Dick would have to go. He lacked the self-awareness, sensitivity, and decorum necessary to lead and inspire a large organization in the midst of a competitive war (deregulation). As one might expect, the chairman was quite reluctant to send Dick home.

He had made quite a statement in hiring Dick. He endorsed him publicly to the media and privately to his board. He committed to an extremely generous compensation package. Nine months into his role, Dick was now known to everyone in the organization. His high-profile image included video conferences, awards dinners, and community executive roundtables. Although feedback about Dick was generally poor, the chairman felt he ought to stand by his protégé. This decision, unfortunately, led quickly to both Dick's and the organization's demise.

As narcissists often do, Dick launched a service-oriented television ad campaign with himself as the star. A series of ads depicted various banking dilemmas in which customers were portrayed as angry and disappointed. Enter Dick on screen wearing a black suit and red tie. He persuasively engaged the viewers in an appeal to switch to his bank as "Service Is Why." This was followed by a promotion to attract new customers.

In his quest for television stardom, Dick had forgotten to notify the internal organization that service delivery would have to be improved to fulfill the campaign's promises. Customers initially flocked to the branches, attracted by Dick's good looks and the sales promotion. However, the service that they experienced was as poor or worse than the industry standard. Teller lines were long; employees were apathetic or rude; the branches were untidy. It did not take long for the Philadelphia business press to capitalize on Dick's debacle.

Once promoted in the media, Dick's doom was imminent. A local business magazine published an exposé of his checkered past, including alcoholism and adultery. The chairman was criticized harshly for his poor judgment in hiring Dick. The public reacted to the media's flagellation by staying away from the bank. Branches were closed and personnel were laid off. Dick was fired and he returned to New York to "pursue other interests." Eventually, what was left of the enterprise was acquired by another bank.

Several years later, I ran into the former chairman at a restaurant opening in Philadelphia. He lamented about the price that he paid for not removing Dick sooner. When I asked him to estimate what hiring Dick cost the organization, he shook his head sadly. "Well," he began, "to get rid of him took well over one million, as he had a rolling three-year contract. But the overall impact is impossible to measure. Reputations, careers, and our image were destroyed in less than three years. The value of the enterprise will never be recouped."

If you choose to do assessment work during the recruiting process, you will begin by interviewing the short-listed candidates. You will be expected to conduct a full character and personality assessment in which they have legally agreed to participate. You will provide a written report that details what you perceive to be the strengths, weaknesses, and potential of each. Finally, you will recommend the top two candidates, or direct the CEO to recruit more desirable possibilities.

Be sure to include a structured interview in your character assessment process. Obviously, personality assessment inventories can be "figured out" by individuals as bright as those you will be screening.

MERGERS AND ACQUISITIONS

Another potential pitfall for CEOs and chairmen is acquiring an organization with a dysfunctional culture. This is caused by self-destructive executives or by a history of poor leadership.

Mergers and acquisitions, though popular, are not often viewed as successful. Four out of five mergers typically fail, and three-fourths of the key executives leave the new organization within eighteen months to three years. Thus, the very assets that were acquired jump ship over time.

A merger typically begins when two organizations agree that together they are a stronger force in the marketplace. There is generally consensus that it is in both parties' best interest to join forces. An acquisition often represents a totally different symbiosis. The acquired organization can feel like a victim or loser, as the new parent now has control over its destiny. There is often tremendous trepidation that it is not "good enough" to have been adopted.

The process in which an organization evaluates its future partner or adoptee is "due diligence." During this process, a team is appointed to intensely study all aspects of the prospect's business: facilities, products, processes services, systems, policies, and performance history. The two areas that can prove to be most elusive are rarely studied in-depth; these are the customers and the culture. Both groups can adversely affect the integration and future functioning of the target.

CDM has often assisted in the due diligence process as subcontractors to investment bankers, venture capitalists, or merger firms. In one example, two computer giants were merging in order to obtain a global market leadership position. While the respective cultures were relatively optimistic about their future vision, both customer groups were outraged and deadset against the move. When we reported this finding, the investment team urged us to get at the root cause of this fury, as it could impede both the merger and subsequent performance of the combined entity.

We discovered through customer interviews with end-users that they feared that the merger would mean a restructuring and downsizing initiative. This could threaten their relationships with project managers who were responsible for automating their outlets. If personnel were laid off, they could lose months having to re-educate a new project team. Understandably, they felt threatened enough to disparage the merger to the media. Through workshops with literally thousands of customers representing key market segments around the world, both organizations were able to "sell" the new vision to its respective customers. CDM's role in analyzing customer's attitudes and then designing an effective intervention to transform negativity was greatly appreciated.

If you choose to support the merger and acquisition process, there are several avenues to pursue. You can be a subcontractor to a due diligence team. You can assist in the announcement and integration process. You can help the new CEO select his top team from merging both executive populations. You can support the reorganization by mentoring the "winners" and "losers."

ORGANIZATION ANALYSES

Organizations are receptive to studying themselves in response to an external force, like global competition, or even the latest management fad such as re-engineering. Most consultancies offer an analysis product whether they focus on business or human processes. While analysis work is fast-paced, short-term, and an excellent entry into other consulting projects; it is exhausting, highly competitive, and typically unprofitable. It is, however, an opportunity for both the corporation and consultant to get to know each other and to determine whether a long-term affiliation is mutually beneficial.

In Chapter 12, I've outlined a suggested approach for conducting an organization analysis as part of an overall culture transformation strategy. Here I will suggest factors to consider in determining whether you would elect to make analyses a part of your product offering.

Analyses are relatively easy to sell if the timing is right. Virtually any new challenge can mobilize an organization to take a closer look at itself. As a corporate therapist, your focus is to assess the organization's capability and capacity for accelerated growth and change. This can be done through a combined approach of confidential, structured interviews and assessment inventories.

In order to ensure reliable data, a critical mass of members ought to participate. Typically, the top five levels are included. Some clients engage in "wall-to-wall" assessments in which each employee is surveyed. Unless you have the technological capability, you will be unable to service such a large population. However, you can conduct a "culture health check" by individually interviewing the top 50 or so executives. You will have to create an interview protocol. A typical analysis approach includes the following topics:

1. Attitudes about the vision.
2. Knowledge about competitive strengths and weaknesses.
3. Awareness of strategy.
4. Opportunities to improve performance.
5. Perceptions about current culture and values.
6. Leadership credibility.
7. Barriers to improving performance.
8. Current and future skill sets needed.

Many consulting firms also examine day-to-day management behavior through "Day in the Life" studies. These involve literally trailing an executive as he conducts his daily meetings, tours plants, deals with customers, vendors, and so on, and then writing up observations of his leadership style, values, strengths, weaknesses, and priorities. Often how he spends his time is evaluated as well to examine his productivity. A clinician's ability to observe dynamics and their implications can be an extremely powerful tool in this kind of study. One has only to read Jules Henry's[1] analyses of families he lived with for a week each to appreciate what can be gleaned through careful observation, documentation, examination and interpretation.

Whether your client is a hospital, law firm, car dealership, or Fortune 100 organization, you can design a protocol that is illuminating. Make sure that your questions provide both quantitative and qualitative data.

CDM typically conducts culture analyses to assess an organization's readiness for culture transformation. We use the assessment

---

[1] Jules Henry, *Pathways to Madness*, (New York: Random House, 1966).

process as an opportunity to build a strong collaborative bond as the basis for future mentoring. Typically, 80 percent or more of our client participants vote "yes" to a pilot mentoring program. If we do not get at least an 80 percent positive response, we would not engage the organization in a culture transformation. Diagnostically, the culture is not prepared or ready for major change.

MENTORING AND EXECUTIVE COACHING

One of the most popular and (easiest to transistion into) services that corporate therapists offer is a mentoring or coaching program for corporations. This is different than a traditional employee assistance program (EAP) in several ways. An EAP is an off-site short-term treatment process for employees who have personal problems (like an addiction to drugs or alcohol). The corporation provides funds for the troubled employee to receive psychotherapy from an EAP provider who has a staff of qualified clinicians. The process is often confidential. Treatment is limited to ten or less sessions.

Mentoring and coaching is done on-site for the purpose of enhancing leadership skills and management performance. The focus is on bottomline results. The program is often linked to operating goals stated in the business plan.

Coaching differs from mentoring in that it is shorter in duration and requires less commitment on both the part of the organization and the corporate therapist. Participation is often optional, because it is not viewed as a systemic strategy for overall culture change. Duration is also optional. Executives may opt to contract for a few sessions or like therapy, the decision to terminate may be made at any time.

Mentoring, on the other hand, requires a deeper commitment. While the executive coach believes the participant is solely responsible for his performance, the mentor, at least as CDM defines it, believes that both he and the mentee are equally responsible. As a growth agent, the mentor must be available upon demand. A typical mentoring relationship lasts at least two years. During that time, an intimate bond is formed in which the mentee is guided, prodded, and disciplined toward breakthroughs in his performance. Stretch goals are envisioned and performance is measured on a regular basis.

While the context of mentoring is different than psychotherapy, the interventions can be quite similar. Chapters 13 and 14 detail both a model for mentoring executives and a sales process. You may find that mentoring a natural next step from an individually-based private practice.

TEAMBUILDING

If you are an expert in working with couples or families, then team-building may be an attractive next step. Quite the management rave these days, most organizations are retaining consultants to help facilitate their team processes and improve their communication in groups.

Facilitating teams is challenging, fascinating work. Multiple realities exist within the team regarding perceptions about the organization. Illusions collide when issues are discussed. Family dynamics, like emeshment, collusion, and scapegoating emerge when debates are at the heart of team members. Roles prescribed in the family of origin (victim, persecutor, rescuer) are unconsciously enacted in the corporate setting as well. Particularly, parentified children present a challenge to the corporate therapist attempting to hold all team members accountable for their own behavior. The defenses of projection, denial, and reaction formation are often in play.

While teambuilding is engaging, it requires a model for both group evolution and team process. The corporate therapist must clearly understand the difference between organizations (acceptance is conditional) and families (hierarchies are fixed). The rules and tactics for closure and confrontation require careful consideration as well. Political realities and professional illusions must be maintained for roles to remain intact. Individual weaknesses must be protected.

At CDM, team facilitation is a part of every mentoring program. At the outset, the team is given a model for optimal team process and the phases of team development. The team then assesses its performance and skills against the model. New skills and strategies for communication are taught and practiced in groups and in individual mentoring sessions. Each member is encouraged to assess his own strengths, weaknesses, and barriers. At the conclusion of each meeting, each team member completes a checklist detailing the team's performance, during the meeting. Confrontation and disclosure are carefully managed. Over time, through the combination of individual and team interventions, the team's process is greatly enhanced. Perception is clearer, problems are faced head-on, and personal responsibility for results is taken.

If you choose to offer teambuilding, be sure to design an intervention that is easy to replicate. You may be a facilitator for an extended period of time or limit your offering to skillbuilding seminars.

SEMINARS AND WORKSHOPS

An effective use of your limited corporate therapy time which can leverage your skills is offering topical seminars and workshops. Easy to design and market, your own line of educational products can be an excellent bridge between private practice and organizational consulting.

While the seminar market is crowded, provocative topics always attracts attendees. Read the business literature to determine what the current interests are. Create a half-day or one-day program initially to build your following. Many attendees will become consulting prospects.

At various times, CDM has been a seminar provider. As I mentioned, I delivered a highly popular workshop for executive women on how to utilize their natural relational abilities in the workplace. We also train clinicians in our consulting technologies. We offer breakfast and supper seminars as part of our culture transformation process to senior executives.

Local television is an excellent medium to promote your seminars. Morning talk shows are always on the prowl for interesting guests with a provocative point of view. You can contact the public relations manager and submit a proposal. If you go on television, ask the station to flash your telephone number on the screen so that viewers can phone to register. I used to go on "AM Philadelphia" and fill up my seminars the same day.

You can also advertise your seminar in newspapers, newsletters, magazines, and computer services. The key is to closely target your market, then offer a specific topic. Often, minorities have special needs that can be addressed best in the seminar format.

OUTPLACEMENT COUNSELING

Certainly there is no faster growing segment in the consulting industry than outplacement. Restructuring and downsizing have created huge opportunities for outplacement firms and corporate therapists alike to help those abandoned resurrect their lives and move on.

The outplacement industry is engaged by the corporation to assist mid- and senior level executives find new employment. Their service typically lasts one year. It is highly task oriented: assessing oneself, preparing a resume, obtaining job interviews, making the short list, and receiving a suitable offer. It is viewed, however, to be lacking the psychological interventions necessary to heal the participant from the trauma of losing his corporate family and identity.

In recent years, outplacement firms have recognized this deficiency. Many top firms are recruiting clinicians to deepen their services. However, you can successfully compete for a portion of their marketshare if you choose not to subcontract your service. The advantage in doing so is that you retain the freedom to design your own intervention as well as manage the quality of your work.

While CDM does not offer an outplacement service, we do mentor executives who have been asked to leave an organization that is a CDM client. Terminations result from both downsizing and poor performance. The mentoring approach is to heal the executive, help him reframe his successes, and support his transition into a new role.

RETIREMENT COUNSELING

The growing popularity of the "second life" movement suggests that a strong market exists for early retirement counseling. Many corporations view this as a threat, but it can certainly be offered privately to the "retail" consulting client.

As more people live longer, there is a trend in beginning second careers or new businesses once initial retirement has taken place. Corporate therapists can design a creative approach to help a young retiree build a new vision, refocus his considerable energy and utilize significant life and corporate experiences.

As you can see, there are many possibilities to creating your service offering and building a product line. In the following five chapters, I will explain in detail how you can approach three specific interventions: transforming cultures, mentoring executives, and studying customers. These are areas in which CDM has developed and delivered specific technologies.

11

Transforming Corporate Cultures

The most challenging and rewarding projects that I have co-designed and co-implemented with CDM chief executive clients have been "wall-to-wall" culture transformation projects. By definition, these include a total analysis of the customers, culture, and business operations; followed by an integrated change program impacting every department and division of the organization. As these projects are psychooperational in nature, they affect both people and processes profoundly. The teamwork and esprit d'corps they generate is both necessary and highly enjoyable.

These large projects typically involve 10 to 15 full-time CDM consultants and 25 to 50 client executives assigned to the project for two to three years. Much work is done over meals and on weekends, in addition to the business day. My role has been to mentor the chief executive and his family throughout the project. The CDM project director manages the consultant team and prepares the progress report detailing key accomplishments and barriers, which he reviews with the CEO twice a month. The mentoring supervisior is a full-time former clinician who oversees the quality of the mentoring program and weekly supervises the mentors in both individual and team sessions. As a result of this integrated approach, the culture and business processes evolve simultaneously.

As discussed earlier, the need for culture transformation grew as chief executives sought to dramatically improve their competitive advantage. This trend started in the early 1980s when external forces such as industry deregulation and globalization occurred. It became evident that an approach for systemic, integrated change was required; and that successful implementation would demand a sophisticated knowledge of people.

I had recently begun taking classes at the Kirschner's Institute for Comprehensive Family Therapy (CFT) as well. These courses, offered primarily to post-doctoral clinicians as part of a certification in CFT, were invaluable in teaching me the PAR model and reparental psychotherapeutic approach. I was quite eager to investigate its utility for corporate culture change. Further, I had done a major research project in graduate school on the psychological development of successful men. This unpublished study clearly illustrated the potential contribution of mentoring in the evolution of highly successful executives.

Over a period of two years (1985–1987) of my own research into the relationship between organization change and individual transformation, I developed the CDM consultancy model I called the "Culture Transformation Process." Within a conceptual framework outlining the phases and objectives of corporate culture transformation, were five stand-alone programs. Taken together, they could produce an overall culture transformation.

Each program in the CDM model corresponds to a particular phase in the culture transformation process. For example, "Customer Analysis" (which leads to a deeper understanding of the psychology of customers) and "Organization Analysis" (a thorough psycho-operational study of the "as is" culture) are front-end phases. They help assess and prepare the organization for transformation. "Mentoring," "Deepening Customer Relationships," and "Teambuilding" are implementation programs. They challenge all aspects of the organization's current approach to customers, business processes, and leadership/performance improvement. The challenge would be to convince chief executives to engage us to do all five programs as part of a long-term transformational strategy.

Much to my surprise, I found the corporate market eager for such a consulting service. As the model had been evolving for two years, prospective clients learned of the benefits of our work from previous clients who had experienced various aspects of our approach. Our work came mostly from referral. The balance grew out of international presentations that I made at various industry conferences which attracted CEO attendees. In addition, through a relationship with IBM, we generated a large number of international financial services institutions as clients. Beginning in 1988, we were engaged in projects in the

United States, United Kingdom, Europe, Australia, and Canada. In 1989, we formally opened our London division.

A wall-to-wall culture transformation generally took three full years to fully implement. To deliver them, we recruited an extremely talented staff of psychotherapist consultants worldwide. To induct them into the world of management consulting, we conducted two-week offsite trainings in which they learned the client's business as well as CDM's specific methodologies. Each project was assigned a full-time clinical supervisor to oversee the mentoring program, as well as a full-time project director to manage the deliverables of the project. Our reputation for doing breakthrough culture transformation work grew with each completed project. Today, we are considered global innovators and leaders in the field of corporate mentoring and culture transformation.

I tell you our story to encourage you to pursue a similar path, if work on a large scale appeals to you. Starting in your local community, you need to do only one large consulting project successfully for referrals to naturally follow. The magnitude of positive business change that these programs generate is indescribable. They also touch people's personal lives deeply. As a result of the bonds that we forge, I stay in touch with clients for years after our project is over. Like being on a battlefield, these CEOs and I have "gone through the war" together and feel a profound kinship.

While you are certainly free to create your own model for organizational transformation based upon your experience, research, and studies, you can also build on our methodology. I envisioned this book to be a guide for clinicians in transition from couch to corporation, so I have included our approach if you choose to utilize it. We have implemented it primarily in large Future 1000 organizations. However, you can apply it to any organization in your local community regardless of size. The phases, dynamics, and objectives of transformation remain the same. The following discussion is an overview of our model and a case study from an actual wall-to-wall culture transformation program.

THE CDM MODEL:
CULTURE TRANSFORMATION: WHAT IT MEANS

Actualizing the corporate vision essentially means transforming the leaders and employees of an organization to be able to transcend their own performance limits, so that breakthroughs in leadership, sales, quality, operating results, and profitability can be achieved. The CDM model integrates operational and organizational change strategies at each management level through building individual and team mentoring relationships with client management. We have found that mentoring relationships are a prerequisite for systemic transformation. CDM's role is to help manage and teach the transformation process, as well as to design an optimal process for ongoing organizational development at the conclusion of the consulting project.

During the culture transformation process, the organization's tasks at all levels are to internalize a higher vision about its potential and how it will conduct business, adopt new values for relating to customers and to each other, demonstrate a leadership style that supports and continually extends the vision, and show dramatic and consistent improvement in bottomline performance.

In directing the organization toward actualizing its business vision, CDM outlines four stages of culture development. Since everyday perception is largely constructed from emotional factors, close attention is paid to how each phase is perceived within the culture. Through these perceptions, we then understand how it impacts the organization on both a macro- and microlevel. This helps determine how to optimally resolve each phase over the specific time frame which is optimal. The developmental stages of culture transformation that we have identified are discussed next.

Transference

This first stage is characterized by the creation of a positive, hopeful, and enthusiastic climate in which people relinquish historical disappointments and reestablish greater trust and dependency upon their leadership. This is accomplished during the first three to six months of the project through the customer and culture analysis processes.

During a customer analysis, a carefully selected group of customers representing all markets and segments are individually interviewed. A video or film of key findings is presented to management and the board. The customer analysis is utilized to test the market viability of the new corporate vision as well as to quantify its potential marketshare, thus set realistic expectations for growth.

The culture analysis follows; it is a structured interview process in which key managers representing the top five management levels individually articulate their strengths, ultimate potential contributions and what they believe must happen for a quantum leap in performance to occur. At the conclusion of this study, the CEO hosts a celebratory event, or series of events. All managers and employees are required to attend. At this time, they are given optimistic feedback and validation regarding their future potential and past successes, as well as videotaped feedback from customers. An overview of the corporate vision, values, and expectations for optimal contribution are presented by the CEO and key leaders. Immediately following this event, a series of positive management changes recommended by participants are rapidly implemented. The positive transference created through this process psychologically "opens" the system for growth, and builds the necessary reciprocity for performance results to be delivered by participants.

During this transference phase, which typically lasts three months, there is a noticeable diminishing of despair, indifference, passive aggression, rebellion, anger, mistrust and disbelief within management in relationship to their organization. This subculture, fueled by positive feedback about strengths and potential impact, is now free to be oriented toward the future vision, and is eager to build on its foundation of successes.

Individual managers freely outline their own successes and how they can further contribute to the future vision. As they are empowered, they assume a greater role as change agents while still operating within the formal corporate hierarchy. A leadership style of unconditional positive regard, positive programming, nurturance, and forgiveness create the cultural climate for macrolevel change. Openness to examining one's strengths along with the struggle for greater success prevails.

Bonding

At this next stage of culture transformation, having established a trusting enthusiastic climate, the culture focuses on learning a new set of beliefs. It examines its values, leadership style, and interpersonal skills. It identifies the gap between current skill sets and those required to deliver the vision. This is accomplished over the next six months. Deepening Customer Relationships Training (DCR), the Mentoring Program and Teambuilding help facilitate the transformation of the top five levels of management, who rolemodel new values and skills to the organization.

Deepening Customer Relationships Training is the CDM program for transforming the sales process and organization. It is designed to actualize the sales potential identified by customers during the customer analysis process. The mentoring program is the "glue" that ensures the success of the transformation process organizationwide. The top five levels of management are supported weekly in managing their own PAR process by CDM mentors. This program helps them avoid the psychological pitfalls of transformation that can undermine the achievement of results. Teambuilding is CDM's program for the facilitation of newly created cross-functional teams constructed for the removal of operational barriers. Trained in transformational dynamics and skills, they learn to utilize a structured problem solving communication process.

These three interrelated programs strategically manage the systemic PAR process and provide the link between individual growth and operating results. During this stage, there is primary emphasis on the horizontal integration of management at the senior level, which creates the solidarity necessary for a new belief system to be accepted organizationwide.

During bonding, the culture is eager to reciprocate having been freed from the constraints of the old system. It actively learns about the vision and defines, by leadership level, what it will take to operationalize it; thus linking vision with business strategy. There is much comparative analysis between past performance and the demands of the future vision. A gradual disclosure of perceived deficits, weaknesses, and lost opportunities emerge. Through cross-functional integration at the top, symbiosis occurs between senior functional leaders. As a result, a strong informal peer network is mobilized among the participating senior executives. Much abreaction in response to the new vision occurs through this system. Mentors have access to this abreactive material, as it is here that insights first occur.

This executive mentee group bipoliarizes as each management level unconsciously assigns symbolic roles to its members. New informal hierarchies are established. Informal leaders who identify strongly with the CEO and mentors act as conduits and champions of the vision. When properly leveraged, they accelerate the change process by promoting it informally and quickly internalizing new values and leadership skills. A second division occurs as those most threatened by the implications of transformation bond as well. Coalitions and destructive emeshments are formed. This group includes the rebels and loners of the organization, and unconsciously assigns them roles to act out resistance and conflicts for the group. Vicariously, each member experiences the impact of leadership decisions as they would affect any member of either group.

Bonding also accelerates the learning rate, as mentoring relationships become firmly established. Positive transference to mentors and the CEO increases as dependency and trust continues to grow.

Transmutation

During this stage, at approximately 12 months, the internalization of a new set of beliefs about the organization and leadership occurs. New interpersonal skills are evidenced which result in performance breakthroughs and behavior change. This happens as a result of a lengthy and turbulent testing phase in which participants experience significant anxiety as they struggle to change. As this new culture is tested for credibility and commitment, repressed conflicts, and fears surface that were protected by performance illusions. Now they are acted out transactionally in the transferential relationships between leaders and their direct reports, and between mentors and mentees. Compulsive repetitious patterns of behavior of historical family origin predominate in an unconscious attempt to maintain the old culture. Through strategic and symbolic re-enactments led by the CEO, senior executives, and mentors, old patterns are transformed into healthy contemporary results driven interactions.

During this stage, there is emphasis on the alignment of new values within each senior executive's functional organization. This helps to create a critical mass of leadership at all levels vertically within each function. Additionally, the Mentoring Program has created interpersonally-sophisticated leaders who accept the regressive trend as inherent to growth. Both of these internal processes—horizontal integration and vertical alignment—create an infrastructure for real and long-lasting organizational transformation.

Within each executive's organization, key changes must be architected and implemented with precision. The utmost coordination and consistency is required to maximize solidarity and minimize resistance. Group strategies are designed in teambuilding sessions, in which executive mentees are assisted in coordinating changes across functional groups.

During transmutation, negative and positive transferences are at their height, as illusions and defenses are discarded. Competition, jealousies, longings, and self-destructive tendencies emerge. The culture unconsciously assigns members in the resistant subgroup the task of dismantling executive leadership. These maneuvers must be predicted and disarmed before they thwart the momentum of the transformation underway.

Self-awareness, as a result of one-to-one mentoring, leads to greater scrutiny of both leaders and mentors. Symbolic events are dissected for hidden meaning and motives. The true level of commitment and belief in the new vision and values is continually tested by the culture. Perception is often distorted, however, through individual's projections.

As recognition increases there is no place to hide from weak performance and poor leadership, hostilities and resentments flair. The culture realizes individually, and through a collective unconscious, growth is now inescapable. While members still seek places to hide, a gradual loss of resistance begins. If enough positive transmutations are engineered by the CEO and mentors, commitment to the new culture is perceived as strong and unflappable.

Members driven to act out resistance and rebellion move into alignment or choose to leave the organization. This symbolizes permission for the organization as a whole to proceed with a full commitment to the new culture. Dogged attention is paid to demonstrating and recognizing new cultural values in everyday practices. A self-legalized morality develops at each leadership level. A second wave of positive transference then builds.

This new culture is articulated enthusiastically to new corporate members. Through its practices, policies, and procedures, processes and teams function efficiently and effectively. However, as greater success at work is realized, personal tensions begin to mount. Individuals express fear they are out-growing their personal networks at home.

Mentees must be groomed to become mentors in order for family bonds to be strengthened. Fears of success, which represent abandonment terror, have lead to greater involvement in work relationships and more distance from family members. By promoting a culturewide therapeutic coalition with friends and family, important supportive relationships are strengthened and commitment to family life is enhanced.

There is full attention paid to this critical dynamic as a part of the overall transformation process, as significant others must be brought along with the change. The culture, familiar now with the necessity of regression as part of growth, recognizes this need for ongoing support in order to continue to grow. The marital unit is promoted as the vehicle for ongoing self transformation. Each mentee receives training in the implementation of the "intra-therapeutic marital coalition," a CFT model which defines the role of the spouses as growth agents and healers for each other.

Launching

This phase entails the embracement of the new vision as a way of life. Full ownership of new values and skills, a personal commitment on the part of each leader to uphold and further the vision and the sense of responsibility to bring others along in their development prevail. This phase begins at approximately 24 months and unfolds for generally one year. During this time, the organization becomes increasingly skillful in observing, monitoring and critiquing its own internal management processes. Individual leaders feel confident in implementing strategies for studying their organizations, measuring and managing change, increasing expectations for performance, and continuing the culture transformation.

This period is characterized by quantum leaps forward in performance, as compared to the transmutation phase, in which it initially appeared to worsen. The final task of launching is to create the "growth management coalition" in which individual leaders commit to supporting each other through regressive trends. This is accomplished by assigning each mentee to mentor two managers who are not his direct reports. The CDM mentors than act as teachers and supervisors to the internal mentoring program.

As empowerment proceeds, the organization seeks to assume its independence. Full ownership for its success is now claimed and dependence on outside consultants diminishes.

During the launching stage, the organization also assumes greater responsibility for its management errors. There is a greater willingness to architect organizational process prior to implementing change. Individuals function with greater flexibility in assuming relational or assertive behavioral styles and analytic or intuitive cognitive styles as needed. There is a strong commitment to generativity and positive modeling and rules for successful relating are closely followed.

As each leadership level assumes the role of ongoing change agent and seeks support at an appropriate level, weaning formally occurs. A final mentoring audit is conducted to ensure the internalization of mentoring is well underway. Recommendations for fine-tuning the program are reviewed with senior management. A model for bringing acquired organizations into the new culture is prescribed.

The success of the culture transformation process depends on a willingness on management's part to play various roles as needed to trigger a response in the culture's development. For example, during the transference and bonding stage, a strong nurturing and positive programming leadership style is necessary. During the transmutation phase, discipline and confrontation predominate.

Initially, losses in sales, inattention to quality, and mismanagement of operations and opportunities are viewed as failures within the culture to integrate regressive trends. Once fusion with the mentors is accomplished and positive programs are internalized, the PAR process begins to move quickly. This results in an accelerated rate of change as well as a decreased tendency to undo success. The relationship between managing growth and operating results becomes obvious to mentees.

At the conclusion of the transformation process, mentees at each level are bonded to each other, thus increasing loyalty and initiative. Change is viewed as an opportunity for growth. Resistance is viewed as inherent to growth and should be consciously processed with supportive mentoring. Benevolence, ethics, and integrity, internalized within each mentee, are reflected in business practices.

At the delivery level, customers perceive the new culture as a commitment by employees to excellence. As a result, the organization gains a competitive market advantage through customer satisfaction and sponsorship and differentiates itself significantly.

The following case study illustrates CDM's culture transformation model applied to a global financial services institution headquartered in the United Kingdom. In this case study, the culture was transformed from a bureaucracy into an empowered system with fluid boundaries. Attention to customer care was the unifying theme driving the business vision and therefore, the culture transformation process.

A CULTURE TRANSFORMATION CASE STUDY

In July 1990, a United Kingdom headquartered global bank retained the services of CDM for assistance in the conceptualization, research, and design of its "Branch of the Future." This branch delivery concept called "Enterprise" was essentially an integrated financial services department store. CDM had demonstrated specialized expertise in incorporating the customer's viewpoint into the organization's vision for competitive advantage. This client sought to ensure market differentiation and customer acceptance of the vision at the earliest design/development stage.

Five studies including individual videotaped interviews were conducted with over 300 hundred customers and noncustomers. A sophisticated psychological understanding of customers' needs, preferences, and resistances was achieved with regard to the positioning, presentation, and delivery of integrated financial services worldwide.

This research was a critical factor in the preliminary physical design of the Enterprise branch, as well as instrumental in the packaging of products, redesigning of services, and redefining training requirements for branch staff. The client's goal was to empower the culture to demonstrate customer service consistent with the Enterprise vision. CDM's research was used to understand how to best integrate the requirements of Enterprise with the development of the bank's employee population.

During the course of this study, it became apparent to the chief executive that for Enterprise to succeed, a critical mass of the bank's management at all levels would need to actively design a culture in which Enterprise could flourish. Toward this end, CDM was asked to conduct a culture analysis, including confidential interviews and group sessions with 150 managers in the head office and field branches.

The findings of the Culture Analysis led to a recommendation for a wall-to-wall organization development project that would include the following objectives:

- To build a culture in which new values, particularly customer service, teamwork, leadership, and recognition, could be internalized and demonstrated in daily operations.

- To establish a horizontally and vertically linked committee/work group process to accelerate and upgrade quality decision making at all levels.

- To instill a customer orientation in servicing both external and internal customers.

- To leverage leadership at each level, beginning with the bank's board.

- To upgrade the quality and efficiency of reporting systems, and design/introduce a feedback loop for management at all levels.

- To integrate the separate domains of culture development, management training, and technical skills training.

- To optimize the performance of "old" culture as it undergoes a transformation to support the new Enterprise vision.

To ensure accountability for organization development, the chief executive assigned dual roles to each of his direct reports to act as head of his functional division and a symbolic leader in the culture. As a result, rapid progress was made in enhancing relationships, clarifying expectations, defining roles and responsibilities, and improving communication and decision-making processes. Essentially, the general managers provided the inspiration, modeling, and permission for the rest of the organization to undergo transformation as well.

Through a series of dramatic moves, the commitment to the Enterprise vision was solidified as sufficient confidence and support was demonstrated at the board and executive levels. The following events unfolded which generated the momentum for a systemic transformation:

- An examination of boundaries and responsibilities of the chairman, the board, and the chief executive, which led to greater trust, enhanced collaboration and mutual respect between the Board and senior management.

- The personal commitment of the general managers to the organization development program that included a commitment for individual mentoring.

- The establishment of a process for two-way communication between the general managers and mentee population, so that performance at all levels could be monitored weekly and continually improved.

- The establishment of the Customer Service Management (CSM) project under the direction of the general manager of

Human Resources. CSM extended the individual weekly mentoring to include approximately 200 key managers. It also included a thorough examination of business processes and reporting systems, a program for optimizing cross-selling and account retention, and the creation of a working group of cross-divisional managers and CDM consultants to identify training requirements for all levels of the bank.

The Mentoring Program was designed so that each weekly session included a module for improving specific leadership skills linked to assessment criteria set forth in the performance appraisal process. Workshops were delivered monthly so that managers could integrate these new skills as a subculture. Feedback about the workshops was presented monthly to the general managers for review.

The rolldown of the Mentoring Program was launched in January of 1991 and audited in June of 1991. The results of this and subsequent audits were very encouraging. The majority of mentees considered the program beneficial; felt a deeper commitment to the bank through bonding with their mentor; and were using their weekly sessions to accelerate the execution of their business plans.

As a result of the first audit, mentoring was expanded to include committee mentoring. In response to negative feedback from several audited mentees, one mentor was quickly replaced. The new mentor worked proactively to preserve the gains of the program and overcome disappointments among these mentees.

As a result of the second audit, conducted in December 1991, the Mentoring program was broadened to include the personnel of the Enterprise branches. Specific modules were developed to establish service quality standards and set "stretch" sales and referral goals. Individual visions for each Enterprise mentee, based on his or her historical strengths, were co-designed by mentor and mentee. Mentees were empowered through self assessment and feedback to actively construct a branch environment in which they could optimally succeed. Considerable attention was devoted to synchronizing the goals of the program with Enterprise business requirements.

The second year of the program focused on divisional mentoring as well as individual sessions. To foster divisional teambuilding, seminars were held with the top two reporting levels in most divisions. Executive teambuilding was facilitated through a mixed venue of Supper Seminars and Away Weekend sessions.

Audit number three was conducted in June 1992. Results indicated that most mentees had achieved their stretch goals and were ready to be launched. Personal development plans including the resetting of stretch objectives were designed.

The final audit was conducted towards the end of the project in January 1993. Again, results were favorable. Some 92 percent of the population rated satisfaction with mentoring as "very good" and "excellent."

Deepening Customer Relationships (DCR)

Special attention was devoted to the staff of the Enterprise project and Enterprise branches, as these two groups represented the future culture of the bank. A two-week CDM training program was delivered to each Enterprise branch to arm personnel with the psychological and operational skills necessary to exceed the financial goals for each branch.

The first of the Enterprise branches was enthusiastically launched in September 1991, following a prelaunch team-build, in which the staff set challenging individual sales and referral goals. They also pledged emotional support to each other in order to "stay in role" while relating to customers during a regression. The new Enterprise branch culture included short-interval financial reporting within the context of a growth-promoting mentoring dynamic. Weekly sales team-buildings were implemented to keep morale high. Performance quickly exceeded expectations; measured by customer satisfaction, increased sales and referrals.

Two additional Enterprise branches launched in 1991 experienced similar success. In year two of the project, three more Enterprise units, which represented the largest financial centers, were opened with DCR support from CDM. In addition, the Enterprise II shops (conversions of smaller, existing branches) were opened. DCR training was customized for delivery to these smaller teams as well.

CDM's DCR program was expanded to encompass the entire population of Personal Financial Managers (PFMs). At the outset, PFM's were generating an average of one fee-earning product per day. Subsequent sales increases of 40 to 60 percent were attributed primarily to DCR training. CDM was asked to expand the training initiative to include a Train the Trainer program and the development of 50 new modules for DCR/Enterprise training.

The financial analysis portion of the CSM project included a lengthy and comprehensive look at financial and operational requirements and existing reporting systems. Facilitated by CDM, it led to the development of base data for measuring individual branch productivity and profitability per full-time employee. This uniform database was revolutionary for this bank as it provided the foundation for bottom-up reporting and goal setting. A methodology for measuring product performance on a monthly basis was designed as well.

A major outcome of this initiative was the Branch Uniform Reporting System (BURS). A Skills Passport and Remedial Action Program were developed to ensure that operational and skills barriers, highlighted through BURS, could be addressed "just in time" through mentoring to impact weekly performance. In addition, capacity and role analyses at the branch level facilitated the development of a system for manpower adjustments and an integrated sales process. CSM Support Sessions helped establish a platform for performance measurement, process management and the setting of service standards. A formal problem-solving system was implemented. This cultural shift was driven by the now system-wide mentoring process.

The Executive committee agreed that it would have taken much longer to progress as fast as it did without CDM's help in engineering a wall-to-wall culture transformation.

The launching initiative began in the second half of 1992 beginning with the conceptual design and development of an internally driven Coaching Program in which CDM mentees could coach managers. The second aspect of launching was the "technology transfer." Managers from the Human Resources Division were trained in CDM's culture transformation model. All participants viewed this training as extremely helpful in understanding the psychological foundation of mentoring. It also helped maintain the integrity of the model as it was applied to other human resources initiatives within the bank.

The final win of the project was the incorporation of the PAR model as a business strategy for annual goal setting. The bank incorporated stretch goals into its formal business planning process. Management fully supported the expectation of a 45 percent performance improvement each year.

As you can see from this case, culture transformation can be a structured, predictable, manageable process for both the corporate therapist and CEO client. It requires psychological expertise, as organizations are similar in their development, structure, and dynamics to family systems. Like the family, corporate life meets profound emotional needs for attachment and identity. As a result, there is a strong inherent drive to reenact emotional conflicts with executive authority figures, using performance as the backdrop. This repetition compulsion is amplified when expectations for performance are significantly raised, thus straining defenses.[1]

Without the recognition that transformation entails elevating standards of performance and therefore has profound implications for intrapsychic functioning, attempts at transforming an organization's culture will fail. The CEO and his direct reports must be engaged in their own self-transformation in order to champion a powerful change process.

In this case, an initial customer analysis project led to a systemic culture transformation, once awareness of the need for change was amplified. It is not uncommon for culture transformation to begin with an initial customer or culture analysis that provides the impetus for change.

---

[1] Alice MIller, *Thou Shall Not Be Aware.* (New York: Collins, 1981).

12

Selling Culture Transformation Projects

O f all corporate therapy work, wall-to-wall culture transformation projects are the most complex. You will need associates in order to implement a program of this magnitude. A typical ratio of staff to client executives is 15 mentees per mentor. You will also need a clinical supervisor who can oversee the quality of the mentoring program. If you elect to embark on the customer analysis and DCR training modules as well, expect to add two more full-time staff. With regard to your own time, expect to devote at least two days a week for client and staff management. Once a Calendar of Activities is completed, you can create reports to help you keep track of progress. Make sure that you obtain a quality supervisor for your mentoring of the CEO. Obviously, you cannot reveal the content of his sessions to your own staff.

If you elect to integrate the operational aspects, you will need to subcontract this work to a qualified operational improvement specialist. Don't be overwhelmed by the project scope outlined here! You can begin this work on a far smaller scale. In your own community, you can identify small to mid-size businesses such as law firms, restaurants, real estate companies, and advertising agencies that require culture transformation. Read the business news each day to identify prospects. Organizations who are acquiring or merging make excellent candidates for culture transformation.

In thinking about what insights that we have that would be helpful to corporate therapists interested in offering culture transformation programs, I thought I might provide answers to the key questions that

CEOs most frequently ask, when deciding whether to undertake such a process. They typically want to clarify:

- ○ What exactly is culture transformation, and how do you change a culture to deliver results on an ongoing basis?

- ○ Are the numbers real, and how does one achieve such significant bottom-line results in such a relatively short time?

- ○ How do you overcome the organization's resistance to change and change agents?

- ○ How do you ensure that culture transformation will last beyond the project and your involvement?

It is important that you provide your prospective CEO client with a conceptual model for culture change that helps justify the investment in such a monumental undertaking. This entails presenting an orderly, sequential flow of activities in which they can insert their own organization's needs and pressing issues.

Further, you will need to explain the link between personal growth and business performance. Within a structured context such as the workplace, gains in personal awareness, insight, and growth can be directly applied to business tasks. However, corporate executives are not trained to see this connection. Typically, there is a clear distinction between what they consider to be the "personal" and "professional" domains.

You will also need to explain the concept of resistance as it is defined clinically. This discussion can include examples of resistance and how your approach can predict and transform it. Resistance is often viewed by executives as negative rather than regressive, and reframing it as a growth trend is useful.

Finally, you must include an explanation of the processes of identification and introjection for the CEO to understand how the transformation moves systematically through formal and informal relationship networks.

Chief executives will expect dramatic improvements in sales, productivity, referrals, profitability, and morale as a result of a culture transformation program. In fact, it is not unrealistic for them to expect the following results:

- ○ A 25 percent increase over previous years operating performance.

- ○ A 35 percent increase in sales productivity.

○ Back-office productivity gains of greater than 25 percent.

○ Improved profitability due to lower operating costs and higher yields and productivity.

○ Employee morale and job satisfaction ratings of "excellent" and "superior."

○ Improvements in quality output, measured by first pass yields.

Also as a secondary benefit, they will expect to be able to merge their organization with others without diluting the new culture that has been put in place.

Before you decide to undertake the delivery of such a program, there are two important prerequisites to consider: (1) Systemic culture transformation will require a major commitment of time, energy, and focus, both your own and your clients; and (2) Considerable soul searching on the part of the CEO is required to design the correct implementation and pace of change. The following four questions may be helpful in assessing whether your CEO prospect is a viable candidate for such a process:

1. Given the current competitive climate, industry positioning, organizational history, and current dynamics, what level of operating results does he require within what window of time to gain a significant competitive advantage? How is a culture transformation program a means to that end? It is not enough to envision and articulate the ideal culture without providing extremely challenging operating goals. Without a direct link between the program and expected results, employees will have no way of measuring the disparity between their vision (which is significantly lower) and the CEO's. Further, programs of this nature require significant momentum and a sense of urgency to offset an organization's natural tendency to return to status quo performance. In fact, an increase of 30 percent to 45 percent over the previous year's operating goals is required in year two, in order to generate the momentum for transformation. Does your CEO have the leadership skills to drive such a process?

2. Given meeting commitments, travel schedules, and professional involvement outside the organization, how much time can your CEO client realistically devote to culture transformation? A well-timed visit from the CEO will have a dramatic

impact on morale. He can often be the catalyst in moving the organization to its next higher level of personal commitment to change. It is important that he devotes enough time to attend organizational events and strategy sessions, and appear unexpectedly where he can observe local cultures first-hand. During these communication opportunities, he can be briefed on what dynamics are occurring so that his message is inspirational and on target. While his time is too valuable to "manage by wandering around," the use of the CEO as an inspirational figure is central to the success of transformation. Employee newsletters, video messages, and personal notes will help leverage his impact but will not substitute for face-to-face contact. Will he commit sufficient time so that such a project is perceived as his top priority?

3. How much freedom does your CEO client have in making changes that demonstrate his commitment to bottom-line? Is he free to recruit and reward executives and eliminate those who are not committed to achieving the goals? Even a senior management team that has been hand-picked will have members whose personal dynamics make them unable to keep pace with the new growth rate. If allowed to act out, they will undermine the program, bipolarize the emerging new culture, and confuse others who are attempting to grow. Not acting quickly to remove poor players sends the signal that he is not serious about results and is giving implicit permission for backsliding. Revitalizing an organization that has drifted back to homeostasis is far more difficult than activating an organization. Does this particular CEO have the "stomach" for removing resisters and saboteurs even if they have been loyal colleagues in the past?

4. Finally, how much effort will it take to move his organization from its current level of performance to a position of market or industry leadership, and what resources can he dedicate to this effort? In order to symbolize solidarity at the top, transformation requires the personal commitment of his senior executives, who must lead the effort down each of their line and staff organizations. A critical mass of leadership must be developed at all levels. Will outside change agents be needed to provide an objective assessment of potential, a blueprint for transformation, ongoing facilitation, and support? Organizations

collude to protect the CEO from the upsetting realities of organizational life by creating performance illusions and filtered reporting systems. Does your CEO prospect have the courage to tear through illusions and overcome what is the typical CEO's existential dilemma?

THE CEO'S DILEMMA

Multiple levels of reality exist within one organization. Implicit agreements and rigid boundaries are in place to keep the CEO from being exposed to true attitudes, skill levels, and performance. As one of my first Fortune 500 CEO clients explained candidly one day, "No one in here wants me to know what is going on—in fact, our whole system is presently structured to keep bad news from my door."

Yet, transformation requires a baseline measure. It is critical that the organization feels secure enough for deficits, barriers, and resistances to emerge, as well as for the root cause of operating problems to be identified. It often takes outside change agents to help the CEO establish an open, trusting system. He may also need support in adjusting to the true realities of performance. These often lurk behind the rhetoric promoted by internal communications and external ad campaigns. Will your feedback be accepted, or as change agent, will you be the messenger that gets shot?

OBJECTIVES FOR A CULTURE TRANSFORMATION PROJECT

The following are key objectives for your CEO client and yourself to consider with regard to planning the scope of a systemic culture transformation project.

Create a Profound Understanding Organizationwide of Customer Expectations, Perceptions, Psychodynamics, and Decision-Making Styles

A customer analysis at the outset of a culture transformation program will test the market viability of the new vision, as well as create awareness and momentum for change. It is an excellent way to build an identification with the customer as the basis for changing the culture. A comprehensive customer awareness program should contain three phases: (1) a psychological study of the customer in each target segment; (2) feedback of findings to all employees through a comprehensive training program; and (3) feedback to the customer regarding the organization's progress and performance. These activities will ensure that the customer's viewpoint is fully integrated into the marketing, sales, design, production, and delivery processes within the culture.

The most common errors in implementing customer programs include utilizing focus groups as a means of gathering crucial data, poorly analyzing and incorporating results into marketing strategy, and not enlisting the customer as an ally, sponsor, and salesperson. All of these can be avoided with proper front end planning and project design.

Understanding the customer's vision for perfect products and services is best achieved through one-to-one videotaped interviews in which the psychological relationship between the customer and organization is extensively explored. Key themes and findings can be explored with senior executives to determine what marketing and sales opportunities can be derived from this input. In Chapter 13, a more thorough approach to studying customers is outlined.

Make a Commitment to Safely Uncover the Truth about Internal Perceptions, Performance, and Potential. Then Set Extremely Ambitious Operating Goals

Once the customer's vision and the CEO's vision are aligned, the next task is to build a shared vision among all levels of the organization. An organization analysis is an excellent vehicle for creating hope and building excitement and momentum. The focus of the study should be on pathways to greater success. Regardless of the business conditions, the communication style should be enthusiastic and optimistic.

Typically, organization analyses offer little insight into the sources of confusion and resistance. They are often viewed internally as a "white glove test" rather than the beginning of an exciting joint venture. Many analyses allow for only forced-choice responses through written surveys and do not provide the participants an opportunity to "dream" or timely feedback regarding overall findings. Typically, findings are not incorporated into strategic planning or day-to-day operations. Further, most consultants do not utilize the analysis as an opportunity to build powerful relationships with client participants. When the analysis is conducted poorly, there is little chance that employees will take much interest in future efforts toward changing the culture.

An organization analysis process should begin with a written invitation from the CEO which outlines the purpose of the analysis, reassurance as to how confidential material will be handled, and dates for feedback sessions for all participants. A working group of key executives can help you design the interview questions and the selection of inventories. Confidential one-on-one interviews are the best method for gathering data as well as for bonding participants to the new vision. Feedback is presented as part of a major celebratory event to discuss findings and next steps. This is followed by written feedback to all participants that summarizes recommendations and commends them for their candor and insight.

The most intensive interviews should be conducted with the CEO, his direct reports, and board members. The next three management levels should be interviewed as well. Lowest-level supervisors can participate in focus groups and all employees can be confidentially surveyed. The questions should be the same for all participants, with particular emphasis on how perceived barriers affect operations and performance at each level.

Findings should be analyzed by level and functional group as input for later horizontal integration and vertical alignment, respectively. The CEO's responses are the model against which other interviews are compared because there are perceptual disparities between the CEO and his senior team. This is not necessarily cause for alarm, but rather indicative of the nature of organizational culture.

Resolving these disparities is a preliminary step toward building a unified culture. CDM has found that many senior executives often disagree as to whom the customer is, therefore marketing strategy gets diluted. Another typical finding is that senior executives disagree how to operationalize cultural values. As a result, many employees feel that there are multiple cultures in place. We often find a schism between strategic planning processes and management by objective systems. For example, "increasing sales" often leads to duplication of effort among line organizations, who in relative isolation take their own customer approach. These conflicts are paradoxes that need to be highlighted and resolved.

In our analysis work, there are three areas of investigation that yield critical findings and produce culture changes. They include an organization's competitive strengths and weaknesses, its cultural values and their reflection in everyday activities, and the perceived potential for optimal performance.

First, we find that many organizations at the senior level do not know enough about their competition, and how it approaches and wins customers. Particularly, little is known about specific products, services, promotions, and key competitor strategies at mid-level management. As a result, at the delivery level, little is known that is helpful in winning a customer from the competition. Yet, this is the level that has direct customer contact. Competitive data is extremely useful in encouraging the organization to develop a warrior spirit in winning marketshare and differentiating itself.

Second, illuminating data comes from a thorough analysis of perceived cultural values. The organization defines what it values (teamwork, trust, recognition, loyalty, communication, etc.), then evaluates how closely the culture reflects stated values in everyday policies, practices, and procedures. Findings clearly illustrate the impact that mixed messages have on daily performance. As a result of values analysis findings, often roles and responsibilities are better defined to support strategic, operational, and cultural objectives.

For example, matrix structures can lead to performance appraisal systems that are viewed by managers as "gang bangs." Performance reports can be seen to confound quality problems. Communication is seen as attacking or projecting blame rather than solving problems. Each disparity between the stated value and subsequent behavior has an operational "price tag." Caution must be used in the presentation of such findings so that a particular functional group is not embarrassed.

An organization analysis process is an excellent opportunity to assess a culture's dedication to its vision. While labeling group members can be a self-fulfilling prophecy, chief executives who are serious about culture transformation make personnel changes sooner rather than later. You might discover character disorders among interviewees that are "red flags." These individuals will need to be closely mentored in order to "keep up" with the pace of change.

Third, it is interesting to ask all participants to define what optimal performance improvement is possible—and how they would measure it if barriers could be removed. Often these estimates are higher than senior management's goals! In a very healthy organization, most participants say that a fifteen to twenty-five percent improvement in bottom-line results is possible, and the probability of achieving it is "very good" to "excellent." This data creates an immediate opportunity for dramatically increasing operating goals. It is also a pleasant surprise to the chief executive, who may be despondent about the sheer magnitude of disparity, illusion, and confusion that gets uncovered.

Analysis findings should be incorporated into a blueprint for culture transformation that outlines operational improvements, training activities, and key projects. The blueprint is then presented by the CEO to all participants in a celebratory manner to empower the organization to achieve its vision.

Support Growth and Deepen Loyalty Through a Corporatewide Mentoring Program

Mentoring is the very heart of culture transformation. In fact, the most costly error organizations make is to attempt to change the culture without effective mentoring in place. This typically leads to the organization privately rejecting the new vision while maintaining an illusion of participation and commitment. The vision becomes an operating reality only when a critical mass of leaders are personally transformed to be capable to deliver it. Without the personal transformation of leaders, the culture change process is viewed internally as one more management fad which will pass over time.

There is a myth within corporate America that mentoring is "something that just happens," and that it "shouldn't be forced." As a result, many corporate mentoring programs are informal, unstructured, and unsupervised. This leads to leaking information, promoting internal politics, encouraging collusions, and using the system as a channel for gossip rather than a vehicle for transformation.

Without a powerful strategic and systemic intervention, there will be no major change in either the culture or the organization's long-term performance. As psychotherapists know only too well, systems without a change agent have an inherent drive to return to homeostasis.

A mentoring program can elevate the image of the institution internally and create a critical mass of leaders at all levels who are personally committed to the organization's vision and goals. The next chapter details an approach for mentoring executives that we have utilized for over 10 years as a reliable vehicle for culture transformation.

Make Training a Constant and Supportive Activity

One of the greatest frustrations of chief executives is the enormous amount of money spent on training programs that deliver few measurable results. Often, training is viewed as an educational requirement having little to do with operations or performance. Corporate trainers lack credibility, as they are poorly versed in operational applications. Off-site trainings do not typically include an assignment to learn the material and deliver it upon return. Most training workshops are not linked to performance appraisal processes, and goal-setting and follow-up are not incorporated into daily management processes. Additionally, the human resource group who delivers training is not positioned as a driving force in implementing business strategy.

In the quest to elevate leadership skills, many organizations have implemented personal growth programs. Groups of managers are taken off-site and encouraged to confront each other with their "true" needs and feelings. As one might predict, these programs produce disastrous results. Boundaries are ignored and personal history is disclosed, shattering necessary social illusions essential for organizational life. As one senior executive confided, "I went to this weekend retreat to have my colleagues tell me what my wife has known about me for years. Now I don't want to get up for work in the morning."

While there is an urgent need to accelerate growth, these kinds of programs are dangerous, as changes in self-awareness are uncontrolled. The web of relationships that each manager is most dependent on is severely threatened. Further, while it is true that most performance problems have their origin in emotional conflict, self-transformation can occur only in a confidential off-line relationship, where image is respected, interventions are focused, and confidential disclosures are safe.

Yet, a major part of transformation is training. To leverage training time, cost, and results, identify training needs for each level and within each functional group during the organization analysis process. To upgrade programs, include a core curriculum and special topical seminars. Encourage each management level to spend the majority of its training time in monthly breakfast or dinner seminars instead of expensive and time-consuming off-sites. Each seminar should include a vision for measurable results and an application for removing cultural and operational barriers. Senior executives should deliver specific modules in order to promote their divisions. The CEO can be used to "kick off" key training programs to symbolize their importance. Programs that make cultural values operational, such as problem solving, meeting effectiveness, coaching, and performance assessment should be mandatory for all management levels. This will help create a uniform culture and leadership style. If outside training packages are used, ensure that they are custom-tailored, with relevant operating examples, role-playing situations, and case studies. Key executives should be encouraged to deliver training to their division rather than relying on outside consultants.

Measure Results against a Standard of Unobtainable Perfection and Continually Raise Goals at All Levels

The essential dynamic in transformation is to raise goals so that they exceed the organizations' "set point" or homeostasis, and then measure and reward results on a short-interval basis. With a mentoring system in place to handle regression and resistance, an organization can take quantum leaps in performance and master the progressive and regressive trends of growth. The key indices relevant to goal attainment must be measured monthly, so that the chief executive can recognize stellar performers on a timely basis.

In many organizations, measurement systems are viewed as inaccurate and information is poorly summarized at each reporting level. Multiple systems often exist due to incomplete systems conversions. Operating goals are not clearly linked to monthly and quarterly performance appraisals and no disciplinary action is taken when goals are missed. Often excuses such as "a slow market" or "tough competition" are acceptable reasons for poor performance.

Discipline is a critical tool in culture change, and constant feedback and support is required for transformation. During the transformation process, managers and employees watch executives closely to determine how much commitment to the new culture really exists. While a sufficient period of time is required for the organization to internalize a new vision, approximately one year into the program, discipline becomes a major leadership strategy and style. Poor goal attainment leads first to coaching and with no significant improvement, to rapid termination.

During the transformation process, bipolarization will occur when individuals realize that change is inescapable. They then decide whether to identify with the CEO or hold steadfast to the old culture and forfeit growth. Those most resistant form a subgroup that unconsciously elects a leader who acts out resistance for the group. This resistor directly challenges the CEO or embarrasses the organization in some way. Conversely, individuals who believe in the vision and are in "positive transference" to the chief executive also bond and unconsciously elect a leader. This champion often achieves a major performance breakthrough—which mobilizes the culture to closely identify with his success and model it.

During bipolarization, the CEO's commitment to the vision is severely tested. Disciplinary action is crucial for the new culture to solidify. If it is delayed, the organization feels implicit permission to return to the old culture and deliver less stressful levels of performance.

Encourage Success and Promote It Widely In-House and to Customers

In the pursuit of modesty, we are culturized to shrug off our successes and scrutinize our failures and disappointments. This dynamic is reflected in organizational life through Management by Exception reporting. Yet, transformation requires encouragement and validation. Positive energy must be injected daily into the culture for employees to solve internal problems and handle irate customers in a positive way. The source of energy that fuels the culture is the constant articulation and abreaction of success.

Feeling successful is typically a reflection of high self-esteem. On an intrapsychic level, the individual targeted for success must be grounded in positive programming ("you can do anything!"); free to make mistakes; and "cradled" during a regressive trend. Most people do not have the ego structure to tolerate much success. As performance increases, negative internalized programs surface to maintain homeostasis within the self system. Regressive episodes are reflected in performance errors. For an individual to transcend ceiling barriers, he must first internalize enough positive programming from a boss or mentor to transmute negative introjected beliefs.

Creating a success-oriented culture begins with noticing, tracking, and talking about success. During CDM's organization analysis process, each participant is asked to recount his key successes in the organization while the interviewer applauds and praises the participant's competence and personal power. This begins the transformation dynamic. Additionally, one of the first tasks of the mentoring program is to interview the candidate at length about his successes throughout the life cycle. Interestingly, we find it very difficult for mentees to stay focused on remembering and recounting successes. Instead there is a tendency to recall failures and disappointments.

In order for success to be internalized, the employee must recount a successful experience in the presence of the mentor or boss who validates it. This articulation can be built into weekly meetings to save time and accelerate growth. Group members, in identification with the employee receiving the validation, are then motivated to increase their performance to be recognized as well. To build mythology, success stories should be included in widely distributed company newsletters. Personalized gifts are also powerful tools for accelerating growth. Symbols such as an expensive tie or briefcase can represent a rite of passage toward becoming a more powerful and successful executive.

Fears of success are, in fact, more potentially self-destructive than fears of failure, as they trigger profound separation anxieties ("Will my peers still like me when I out-perform them?") Generally during culture transformation, employees are actually discouraged by friends and family who guard particular barriers to success. Therefore, the family should be encouraged to support the transforming organization so they do not feel threatened and unconsciously sabotage its success.

Engage the Media as an Ally

Culture transformations often attract the attention of the business media. Without a proactive press strategy, the organization is vulnerable to the media's evaluation of the program before it has a chance to deliver results. Often programs are damaged by a premature negative press reaction that disheartens employees and discourages customers. A key tactic is to enlist a public relations expert who has extensive industry experience and excellent press relations.

An effective public relations program should begin with a media analysis and a press audit in order to identify a target list of key publications, potential press relationships, newsworthy products and services, and a blueprint for press conferences, interviews, promotions, and marketing and advertising strategies.

A precise narrative describing the organization's vision and transformation program should be documented and distributed to key executives to ensure uniformity of messages to the press. A media training session can be useful to ensure that communication with the press is uniform and limited to the chief executive and a few senior executives who clearly embody the new cultural philosophy and style.

The CEO's image is of critical importance in building sponsorship and credibility with the media. It is helpful to videotape a CEO press interview, and then scrutinize it with him to ensure that powerful bonding techniques are integrated into his overall message and stance.

While many CEOs view the media as a "necessary evil" and take a reactive approach, the media can quickly transform the organization's image. Enlisting the media as an ally helps decrease the risk of unexpected or negative exposure. This step should be taken before a culture transformation program is well underway.

Hopefully, these objectives can help on both selling and delivering culture transformation programs. Next to the bond between yourself and the CEO, planning these myriad activities will be your top priority. Constructing the "blueprint" in which activities can be then organized and integrated can take several weeks of upfront time.

In the following chapter, we will examine how mentoring can be utilized as a vehicle for systematically transforming the culture on both a macro- and microlevel.

13

Mentoring for
Accelerating Growth

B y definition, culture transformation requires a faster pace of
growth for the organization and therefore the individual. This
means that its subprocesses including progression, regression and abreaction, must move more quickly. In addition, it requires pressure on all
fronts in order for there to be no place to hide. It also needs ongoing
momentum for a breakthrough to occur. A breakthrough, defined as
performance consistently above the ceiling limit, will ensure that the
"set point" or homeostasis, will stabilize at a significantly higher level.

Given these requirements, it would seem that accelerating growth
would take a highly structured, engineered process; in which various
growth-promoting stimuli could trigger particular responses. In order to
know what stimuli would optimally create various growth-enhancing
reactions, the growth process must be clearly understood.

APPLYING THE PAR MODEL

The PAR model, detailed in Chapter 5, makes mapping such a process
possible when applied to the growth of corporate performance. This
application initially had tremendous significance for the typical
client/consultant contract. Historically, management consultants sold
their services either on the basis of a one-time 15 percent performance
improvement or a 3:1 annual return on the investment in fees. There
is certainly nothing transformational in that. However, with PAR as a
roadmap, corporate performance could be engineered to significantly

137

higher levels. If transformation is the goal, then a minimum of a 35 percent improvement in performance would be targeted in order for a breakthrough in homeostasis to occur.

In speaking at length on several occasions with Drs. Kirschners and Stein, I became quite eager to utilize the principles of PAR in engineering culture transformation. A pressing challenge for my chief executive clients was leading a culture transformation process. I felt compelled to alert them to the potential of applying PAR to this corporate task. The final result of our PAR application to culture transformation is illustrated in Figure 8.1.

CDMs model applies the principles of PAR to a two-year corporate evolutionary process in which culture transformation is the goal. Through engineering growth, thus stimulating both progressive and regressive trends, a series of breakthroughs in performance occur. While this model can be applied to engineer virtually any kind of performance improvement (e.g., productivity, sales, quality, profitability), a commitment to deliver performance at a 35 percent increase is essential in triggering sufficient progressive/regressive oscillation.

In applying the model initially to mentoring my own chief executives, it became obvious that particular progressions in goal-setting triggered typical regressive responses. For example, a commitment to deliver a 15 percent performance improvement led the client to ponder, "Is this actually possible, and if so, why hadn't I thought of it myself?" This regression was termed "introspection."

A 25 percent performance improvement led to more profound regressive phenomena. Once achieved, the individual insisted that this new performance level could not be sustained. He believed the environment was responsible. As such, his performance was not controllable by himself. With subsequent abreaction of examples in breakthrough historical performance ("Well, I was number two in my graduating class . . ."), the individual integrated this new achievement into his self-concept and was ready for higher pursuits.

The commitment to deliver performance improvements of 35 to 45 percent, however, brought forth the deepest intrapsychic conflicts within the self. It appeared that the subselves were debating whether this was such a good idea! From an object relations perspective, the introjects and the deeper self were engaged in warfare to preserve the territory of the ego. A breakthrough required that a new identity be forged. This regression, characterized as "fear of success" took many forms including depression, acting out, running away, self-destructive behavior, negative transference and passionate, raging, argumentative debate. In whatever expression, it required that the death of the old self be faced and a new identity be consciously acknowledged.

Once the new self was solidified through an ongoing abreactive process of articulating this internal debate and eventual grief, the individual suddenly lightened up. The attitude that, "having survived this battle, now anything is possible," emerged. This final regression was termed "integration." At this time, baseline performance was considered quite substandard, and set point performance was considered merely the current step in a limitless evolutionary process.

Experiences of self transcendence often accompanied this "integration" and set the stage for independent ongoing self-transformation. At this stage, the individual was often motivated to turn to meditation or religion as a vehicle for continued self transformation, as well as to their spouse as an at-home growth agent and healer.

While the entire PAR cycle could occur several times daily depending on the task, overall self-transformation took quite a bit longer. Empirically, the introspection phase took as long as three months and resolving fear of failure took appropriately three months. A breakthrough could take as long as one year. Consolidation took three to six months as well. After experimenting with the PAR model in my own corporate therapy practice and reviewing results in regular clinical supervision, it seemed that an engineered transformation through accelerating growth could be minimally accomplished in about two years of weekly mentoring of a highly motivated client. After that, the client could continue his self-transformation process without a formal mentor.

In designing a corporate application for accelerating the PAR process, several assumptions were accepted:

○ Growth would require a growth agent who could reliably provide growth-promoting stimuli and experiences and facilitate the self discovery process.

○ The total bi-phasic growth dynamic would require emotional support and strategic management, as regression was abreacted in the context of a therapeutic relationship.

○ The pace of change, while challenging, could not exceed the individual's maximum tolerance for growth, therefore cause fragmentation or unnecessary rejection of the process.

- ○ The client would have to willfully engage in such a process and trust the facilitator's know-how.

- ○ There would need to be a reliable map of the interior psyche to determine the impact of various stimuli on subsequent responses.

This led me to examine relevant psychodynamic theories and models in order to clearly understand how PAR impacted the intrapsychic system (see Bibliography). My own transformation process and client descriptions of their changes in awareness were considered as well. The resulting "levels of self" personality model that was developed is illustrated in Figure 13.1.

This CDM model conceptualizes the self as occurring simultaneously on ten connected levels of consciousness, in which perception moves successively from an external to internal focus. Awareness and mastery of each level is the goal of self-transformation. As each level is consciously perceived and examined, the opportunity to go deeper becomes possible. Just by incorporating each level into awareness, the transforming individual achieves mastery, as he now has free choice in

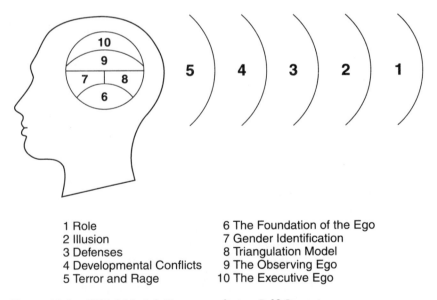

1 Role	6 The Foundation of the Ego
2 Illusion	7 Gender Identification
3 Defenses	8 Triangulation Model
4 Developmental Conflicts	9 The Observing Ego
5 Terror and Rage	10 The Executive Ego

Figure 13.1   CDM Model Conceptualizing Self-Consciousness as Occurring Simultaneously on Ten Adjoining Levels.

accepting or rejecting each level. It is also believed that the journey through the ten levels requires a trained facilitator to provide nurturance, acceptance, enactment and direction. Once the "self" level is achieved, infinite levels of awareness become possible through a direct connection with the universe as constant teacher.

The facilitator is viewed as a guide as well as healer and energy source, as grounding and strengthening the inner self is often necessary to risk this inward journey. This facilitator must be far along in his own self-transformation to be an effective guide and interpreter. It would seem that the most obvious "pool of talent" for facilitators could come from specially trained psychotherapists already clinically and academically familiar with intrapsychic phenomena and their behavioral manifestations.

While some awareness of all levels is possible, full awareness of each level occurs sequentially over time. Facing each level requires greater and greater mastery of the "terror of the unknown." It is only when level 10 (self) is achieved, terrors diminish with the recognition that the self cannot be destroyed and is infinite. What was believed to be the self is only the ego, which is a necessary but limited apparatus for operating in the world.

The levels of consciousness evolve, and are arranged to protect the inner self from both real and imagined danger in the physical world. The greater that consciousness is focused externally, the greater the distance to the self there is to overcome. Moving outward to inward demands increased risk and exposure, as each level moves closer to the ego core, where fear of annihilation is greatest.

As gatekeepers to the ego's core, each level represents a layer of self-protection. "Illusions" for example, protect the unconscious self from mobilizing costly defenses. The level of "defense" protects the self from the anxiety of conflicts. The "conflict" level is the behavioral manifestation of avoiding ambivalence and also contact with one's deepest terrors. The "terror" level is the final level of self protection against direct damage to the ego foundation, in which fragmentation could result in actual psychosis.

The personality structure in this model is viewed as dynamic, growth seeking and permeable to helpful input. The levels of consciousness thus represent access channels and arenas for transformation. Starting with the outermost level shown to the world leading into the innermost core of the inner self where core beliefs, impulses, spirits, and genetic potentials reside, they include the following levels.

CDM'S LEVEL OF SELF-CONSCIOUSNESS MODEL

Level One—Role

The person as he defines himself by social/cultural symbols and criteria including gender, title, degrees, financial status, marital status, and so forth. These symbols communicate meaning to non-intimate observers regarding the outward presentation of self. This level is consciously constructed.

Level Two—Illusion

The set of misperceptions the person holds as beliefs regarding life, death, success, power, health, wealth, happiness, love, achievement, leadership, and so forth. Illusions are negative assumptions learned in the family and reinforced in the popular culture. Unconsciously accepted, thus unchallenged, they stand in the way of courageous action toward self-transformation. They must be transmuted in order for growth to occur (e.g., "Nobody's marriage is ideal." or "You can't have it all."), yet direct confrontation of them will result in an "argument" with their owner.

Both these levels comprise the "false self" personality presented in everyday life. In most people, full conscious awareness of the eight deeper levels stops here. In fact in most corporations, understanding causes of performance barriers stops at the illusion level. This is why organizational change is often short-term and rhetorical rather than transformational and results-driven. When deeper barriers remain hidden, the organization remains "safe" although inaccessible and indifferent to major change.

The following eight levels can be accessed through facilitating a powerful and strategic process of self-discovery, in which a therapeutic relationship forms the foundation for transformation.

Level Three—Defenses

The level in which a person unconsciously guards against disappointments, anxieties, conflicts, and changes that exceed his acceptable pace. Defenses are autonomic reactions outside conscious awareness, and must be strategically elevated to be penetrated and confronted (e.g., "He did that to you!" or "Well, you couldn't have known!") Strengthening the deeper self also reduces the need for self-defense. Defenses are barriers to effective and objective decision-making and leadership. As such, they become more "costly" as responsibilities increase. Some common psychoanalytically based defenses seen frequently among executives[1] include:

- *Intellectualization:* An over-reliance on logic and analysis and discounting of intuition or emotion as a source of learning. This "schizoid defense" has led major corporations to "misfire" as a result of inaccurate perceptions regarding opportunities or challenges.

- *Denial:* Seeing only parts of reality that confirm the self's internal belief or illusion system, which leads to blind spots and muted sensory experience. In leaders, denial often results in underling sabotage or in exposure of the organization to unforeseen danger.

- *Fantasy:* The retreat into an internal world to avoid difficulties of corporate life. This leads to grandiose, unachievable visions. "Magical thinking" is also common, and is a combination of denial and fantasy (as found in the narcissistic defense).

- *Projection:* Assigning positive and negative characteristics onto others that the self is not strong enough to own. In corporate life, subordinates are often over—or undervalued based on leaders projections, which then lead to unrealistic performance expectations.

- *Displacement:* Acting out emotional upsets inappropriately rather than threatening a powerful transferential relationship. This is commonly done by expressing rage or frustration against a subordinate or customer which is actually felt toward the boss or organization.

- *Altruism:* Acting in overly generous or benevolent ways as a strategy to avoid underlying conflicts. Insincere altruism is

---

[1] George Valiant, *Adaptation to Life: How the Best and Brightest Came of Age,* (Cambridge: Harvard University Press).

evidenced in leaders who devote time and resources to social causes instead of nurturing relationships at work or at home.

○ *Repression:* "Forgetting" hurtful experiences from the past which then causes them to be repetitively reenacted[2] with powerful figures in the present. Most often, corporate reenactments are situations in which power and intimacy are inappropriately managed, such as the classic role reversal of boss and subordinate.

Level Four—Developmental Conflicts

Conflicts are behavioral expressions of emotional ambivalence that present a major challenge in maintaining a consistent leadership style. Unresolved emotional conflicts lead to developmental arrests that are characterized by repetitious cycles of approach/avoidance behavior. As defined by Erikson[3] they include conflicts in attachment, trust, autonomy, responsibility, industry, identity, intimacy, generativity and ego integrity. Conflicts must be correctively reenacted in vivo in order to be optimally resolved. In this model, the validation and acceptance of the homeostatic pole of the conflict ("Of course you can't trust me") leads to a morphogenic (growth-oriented) trend ("But I want to trust you"). Successive, fulfilling reenactments promote positive change and integration. As conflicts are resolved, greater energy and creativity is freed up for leadership.

Level Five—Terror and Rage

The last protective layer guarding the inner self structures, it is often displayed as sudden movements toward or away from powerful intimate others. Negative childhood experiences, unexamined and unresolved, have created these deep states of unconscious terror. The five basic terrors represent profound fears of power and intimacy. Terrors are acted out impulsively in an unconscious hope that through repetition they can be mastered. They include:

---

[2] Alice Miller, *Thou Shall Not Be Aware* (New York: Basic Books, 1984).
[3] Erik Erikson, *Childhood and Identity* (New York: W. W. Norton, 1950).

- *Abandonment:* The sense of impending uncontrollable loss; often experienced as a feeling of invisibility and insignificance in relationship to others.

- *Engulfment:* The sense of suffocation; experienced as grief at losing the self and rage at feeling overpowered by others.

- *Entrapment:* Expected deception or betrayal experienced as a fear of being manipulated, exposed, or controlled by others.

- *Rejection:* The expectation that true needs will be unmet and that exposing them will result in humiliation.

- *Annihilation:* A sense of danger or possible death as a reaction to previous emotional or physical abuse.

In this model, it is believed that abandonment terror (separation anxiety) and engulfment terror (sublimating one's needs to please others) exist in everyone while degrees of other terrors may exist as well. The conscious awareness and mastery of terror, including the enactment of rage and mourning for the damaged self, are crucial milestones in the actualization of the inner self's full potential.

Terrors are released through reenactments with positive outcomes, the symbolism of strategically regulated distance and closeness; and through receiving continued support during an attempt to destroy an important relationship.

Levels six through eight represent the deeper self-system, which includes three subsystems that are in constant dynamic exchange.

Level Six—The Foundation of the Ego

Born out of positive contact with the original parenting figures, it contains basic self-love, genetic potentialities, well-being, hope, spirit and eagerness for growth.

Level Seven—Gender Identification

The sense of basic femaleness and maleness broadened to include the range of emotional and instrumental behaviors for establishing relationships and mastering tasks, respectively.

Level Eight—Triangulation Model

The learned paradigm for relating in groups of three or more, based upon one's role prescription[4] in the family of origin. These early experiences establish a blueprint for later corporate teamwork.

Levels nine and ten are developed or strengthened as a result of the self transformation process:

Level Nine—The Observing Ego

The ability to monitor one's own behavior with a realistic eye. It is particularly useful in leadership situations in which one's impact must be accurately gauged.

Level Ten—The Executive Ego

The part of the self that can oversee and direct an ongoing internal transformational process in which barriers can be observed and then transmuted.

FUELING THE SELF

Once the observing and executive egos are seeded or strengthened, the self system is fueled by will. Will is viewed as a limitless energy source that springs from a direct connection to the universe.

Mapping the interior psyche provided a roadmap and strategy for engineering the transformation of consciousness. Various levels of consciousness could be observed in action, then mirrored for the transforming individual. Learning how to best bring about awareness also highlighted the need for an indirect strategic approach. For example, increasing awareness of a particular level requires focusing on the level below it. If the goal is the awareness of a conflict in basic trust, for instance, the individual is prized for his healthy fear of intimacy. This then leads to exploring the reasons why trust is a complex issue that requires careful conscious deliberation:

---

[4] Kantnor and Lear, *Inside the Family* (New York: Harper Colophon Books, 1976).

FACILITATOR: "Given your background, you certainly learned to watch out for yourself at a young age. How did you avoid getting conned?"

CLIENT: "Well, of course, I learned to rely on my own instincts."

FACILITATOR: "Well, thank God you had the wherewithal to survive, living as a street kid in a sense."

CLIENT: "Obviously, it was not always easy to get along on my own."

FACILITATOR: "Not to mention the loneliness you had to feel."

CLIENT: "Well being alone is certainly better than winding up dead."

FACILITATOR: "Absolutely. However, now you have the experience and confidence to determine who can and can't be trusted as an adult, instead of a child."

CLIENT: "Well, it's not quite that simple."

FACILITATOR: "It's extremely difficult for all of us to not confuse the past with the present, but it certainly is a learnable skill."

Further experimentation using this model to facilitate consciousness led to appreciating how futile verbal confrontation would be. Inappropriate interpretation, for example, would lead to strengthening the resolve to maintain rather than transform a particular level. For instance, the stimulus "You are denying!" will inevitably be followed by the response "I am not!"

Working indirectly, however, a comment such as, "It must have been quite difficult to find yourself as an adolescent without parental support" leads to a response such as "Well, I don't think I ever really have found myself" (thus exposing a conflict in identity).

To accelerate conscious awareness, communication is used as a highly strategic process. The dialogue below illustrates how all levels are acknowledged and indirectly exposed within the framework of building a vision for retirement:

FACILITATOR: "Have you thought much about retiring?"

CLIENT: "Well, you know, one day you get old and die." (Illusion).

FACILITATOR: "Right. We can certainly depend on death and taxes (validates and elevates illusion). But many people actually fear leaving their jobs."

CLIENT: "Not me. I'm going to sit back and watch the grass grow." (Denial, defending against conflict in generativity.)

FACILITATOR: "If you could have the perfect retirement, is that what it would look like?" (introduces progression)

CLIENT: "What difference would it make? It won't happen!" (conflict in industry)

FACILITATOR: "Why is that? You know, I am very willful. . . ." (assumes symbiosis with client)

CLIENT: "Yeah, right. Well, I guess I would start up a little crafts shop, but it probably wouldn't be successful." (Conflict in identity)

FACILITATOR: "You would spend how much time there?" (presses on, ignoring self-doubt)

CLIENT: "I'd probably live there!" (conflict in intimacy)

FACILITATOR: "You could put in a sofa bed, microwave, and bar size TV!" (supports homeostasis of conflict)

CLIENT: "Anything to keep me out of the house." (Engulfment terror)

FACILITATOR: "Well you know, a man's true sensuality comes out after sixty." (Ignores terror)

CLIENT: "Not with my wife, it won't." (Abandonment terror)

FACILITATOR: "Let's make her into a hot tamale. That's a worthwhile goal." (Introduces progressive goal)

Once this model had been utilized empirically as a tool for understanding client consciousness and behavior, it became apparent that the therapeutic relationship required for transformation needed special definition and standardization as well. Designing such a relationship led to re-examining the potential of mentoring as a possible dynamic.

As a graduate psychology student, I conducted a series of research studies into the origins of success among executives. Executives of varying ages (from 28 to 60) were interviewed at length. Surprising to me, they consistently attributed their success to a profound relationship with a mentor. The mentor was described similarly as an inspirational figure who was a trusted, confidential advisor; an expert in a technical capacity; a person of integrity and fine character; someone who was available for help in a crisis; a respected authority figure and a role model in general. Mentors took the form of sports coaches, professors, bosses, military leaders, or family friends.

These relationships were basically characterized by a healthy rapprochement process. The executive internalized the life stories and teachings of his mentor. Once fueled, he entered the world more confident and eager to make his mark. When his path became obstructed, he returned to his mentor for assistance and inspiration. Those interviewed attributed their quick ascent as an outcome of this highly valued relationship.

The mentor became introjected as well. Years after contact, these executives still believed, "Oh, of course, I could pick up the phone and call him right now. Wherever he is in the world, he'd get right back to me."

In examining the intrapsychic dynamics of this relationship, it appeared that emotional learning took place which was far more efficient than experiencing life's challenges on one's own.

Through an identification with the mentor's success, the executive felt empowered to dream and achieve a vision that represented a quantum leap in growth. The rapprochement dance between mentor and mentee provided a safety net for his ongoing regressions. Over time, through the symbiosis established between mentor and mentee, the executive introjected parts of the mentor that were useful in fulfilling his own vision. Through the process of projection, he perceived the world as receptive to his talents and dreams. As a result, he "organized" the environment to nurture his accelerated growth. Feeling gratitude for the mentor's assistance, he sought opportunities for generativity with less experienced colleagues. For that, he was viewed by others as having leadership potential. The net result of this process was rapid career promotions.

The findings of these studies, although not formally published, led me to wonder, if transformation within the corporation required a rapid pace to ensure competitive advantage and would need to be engineered, who would be competent to direct and manage such a process? And, if mentoring had proven empirically to result in greater corporate success, could it be formally designed to transform executives? Finally, given the politics, illusions and hierarchies of corporate life, how could mentoring be defined so that individual vulnerabilities would be protected?

Pondering these questions led to the design of CDM's mentoring technology. It includes a two-year weekly process in which a CDM psychotherapist-consultant delivers a series of structured modules to an executive mentee. It also includes a monthly seminar in which groups of mentees are educated about mentoring others. The Mentoring Program became operational in 1987, and consistently generates two-thirds of CDM's annual billings. It has become the cornerstone of our approach to culture transformation.

THE PROCESS OF MENTORING

Figure 13.2 depicts the overall CDM schema for the mentoring process. As a result of observing and identifying various interpersonal and intrapsychic dynamics and events, specific mentoring activities have been designed that trigger or accelerate growth through a transformation of consciousness. Mentoring occurs in five interpersonal phases which unfold over the two years.

Phase One: Testing
(Transformation of Self-Esteem)

On an interpersonal level, the mentee moves through distinct phases of relationship to the mentor. During the initial "testing" phase, the mentee assesses whether the CDM consultant is "good enough" to act as his mentor. The mentor is tested in many symbolic ways:

- The mentee reveals confidential material, then has a colleague attempt to organize the mentor to repeat it.

- The mentee gives the mentor various documents to review in the hope that the mentor can make a valuable contribution.

- The executive attacks the mentor as incompetent, as he is not a specialist in the client's business or industry.

On an intrapsychic level, the executive mentee is bipolarized, feeling a combination of infatuation ("This mentor is really just for me!") and suspicion ("What if what I say ends up in my personnel file?"). Self-disclosure and awareness is initially limited to the role and illusion levels of consciousness.

It is the task of the mentor to build enough positive transference for growth to occur. He does this proactively by engaging the client to examine the successes throughout his life, beginning with early childhood memories and moving forward chronologically. This process (detailed on page 70) culminates in an extensive analysis by the mentor of the mentee's core strengths. These are communicated in a specific format (both face-to-face and in writing) in a way which promotes a transformation of the mentee's self-esteem.

This testing phase takes between five weeks and three months (depending upon whether the client has engaged CDM to deliver its full two-year program, or the shorter term counterpart, Accelerated Growth Learning System).

Phase Two: Transference (Transformation of Acceptance of Potential)

The second interpersonal phase "transference" begins with the completion of the Success Interview process. The mentor is now perceived as worthy and having earned the right to examine the mentee in other ways. At this stage, intrapsychically, the mentee is feeling the longing to surrender to authenticity, as well as defensiveness in exposing his true weaknesses and deficits.

The mentor's key task for accelerating growth at this phase is to engage the mentee in a creative application of his core strengths. He does this helping the mentee envision his ultimate contribution to his corporation, family, health, sport, and (taken together) recreational and life retirement goals. This four-quadrant approach provides the pressure on all fronts necessary for transformation. In each quadrant, past performance is reviewed as a baseline for goal setting. A vision which represents a 45 percent performance "stretch" is architected. Measurements are creatively designed to fit particular goals ("10 perfect forehands before a ball miss").

The conclusion of this stage culminates in a transformation of recognizing one's true potential. The mentee agrees to "experiment" with self-transformation by attempting to actualize the various quadrant visions with the ongoing support of the mentor. This phase takes between six weeks and three months.

Phase Three: Symbiosis (Transformation of Personal Power)

In the third interpersonal phase termed symbiosis, the bond between mentee and mentor is deep, however it is limited to a shared commitment to actualize the mentee's visions. In pursuit of the higher levels of

Interpersonal Relational Stage (The Dance of Relating)	Intrapsychic Consciousness (Self-Perception and Dialectic)	Mentoring Process Step (Growth Triggers)	Time Frame (Internal Changes)	Mentor's Tasks (Transforming the Candidate)
Testing ○ Confidentiality ○ Flexibility ○ Strength/power ○ Androgyny ○ Stability ○ Sexuality ○ Ethics ○ Vulnerability ○ Intellect ○ Commitment	**Role/Illusion (and Suspicion/Infatuation)** ○ Compartmentalization ○ Rationalization ○ Acting out	**Creative Approaches/Reframing History** ○ Observation ○ Synchronicity ○ One-upmanship	**3 Mo.** Awareness of deeper self →	○ Creating the role ○ Building the transference ○ Hurdle jumping ○ Differentiation from historical transference figures
Transference ○ Technical ○ Intellectual ○ Symbolic ○ Emotional ○ Sexual	**Defense (and Surrender)** ○ Intellectualization ○ Denial ○ Projection ○ Reaction formation ○ Altruism ○ Repression ○ Fantasy ○ Grandiosity	**The Success Interview** ○ Unconditional positive regard and specific positive feedback	**6 Mo.** → Integration of subselves	○ Regression ○ Analyzing successes and creation of a hopeful, integrated future ○ Positive reframing of historical failures ○ Future visions for love, success and power

Symbiosis
- Hypersensitivity
- Danger zones
- Mirroring
- Reenactment
- Interpretation

Transmutation
- Symbolism
- Paradox
- Architecture
- Grief/mourning

Transformation
- Emotional
- Cognitive
- Physical
- Relational
- Intellectual

Conflict (and Longing)
- Attachment
- Trust
- Power
- Responsibility
- Sexuality
- Identity
- Intimacy
- Generativity
- Integrity

Terror (and Passion)
- Engulfment
- Entrapment
- Annihilation
- Abandonment
- Rejection

Self-Will (and Break-down/Indifference)
- Establishment of will
- Perception of reality
- Actualization of self

Observing ego →

Creating a Shared Vision
- Work through repetition compulsion and developmental conflicts

Executive ego → 18 mo.

Expectation Setting
- Programming and cognitive restructuring

24 Mo. Alignment of behavior →

Launch and Transfer
Transfer process to:
- Spouse/children
- Colleagues
- Underlings

- Provide positive inputs
- Interpretation of behavior based on history and programming
- Establish true emotional age
- Construct experiences and enactments to resolve developmental arrests

- Extend ceiling limits
- Attack introject negative beliefs
- Challenge life script
- Metaphors and alternate life philosophies
- Integrate self parts into Observing Ego

- Establish new emotional age and life role
- Identify person as change agent
- Begin marital reconstruction
- Workthrough termination

Figure 13.2 CDM Mentoring Model for Self-Transformation.

performance demanded by the quadrant vision, the mentee experiences profound intrapsychic conflicts. These are unconscious and evidenced symbolically though behavior.

The mentee "organizes" the mentor by enacting various compulsive repetitious patterns learned in the family of origin (e.g., caretaking attempts toward the mentor). While these are viewed as unconscious attempts at mastering dysfunctional patterns, it is the mentor's job to ensure that mastery over these impulses actually occurs.

The mentor's key tasks at this phase are to provide positive programming and helpful strategies for achieving the vision, as well as interpret conflicts as they occur. Mastery is achieved through corrective enactments (e.g., caretaking of the mentee and refuses any gestures of this kind in turn) creatively engineered by the mentor. Further, the mentor introduces a series of skill-building tutorial modules specific to achieving the mentee's vision (such as presentation skills, conflict resolution, confrontation skills, etc.). These help decrease the performance anxiety and frustration characterized by conflicts in general.

This phase culminates in a transformation of personal power. The mentee recognizes he is free to respond to the world in any way he chooses and is not constrained by experiences from the past. Defenses such as projection and displacement become unnecessary when anxiety and ambivalence can be faced head on. This activity is ongoing from six months into the second year. However, successful re-enactments quickly lead to a deeper mentor/mentee dance.

Phase Four: Transmutation
(Transformation of Self-Love)

During the transmutation phase, the fortitude of both mentee and mentor is severely tested. Fears of successes have become activated as a result of a continual progression in performance. It is at this critical juncture that the mentoring relationship is the most fragile, volatile, and pivotal for future self-transformation.

The mentee demonstrates that transmutation is occurring through exhibiting behaviors that symbolize terror. If abandonment is feared, the mentee will attempt to terminate the relationship. If annihilation is what is dreaded, the mentee will attack, humiliate, and otherwise attempt to "destroy" the mentor. If entrapment is feared, paranoid fantasies involving betrayal with a third party predominate. If engulfment is feared, the mentee will "go underground." Rejection leads to inappropriate intimate advances toward the mentor.

Feeling passionately committed to his visions, as well as terrified that they may actually become real, the mentee also attempts to self-destruct. He may threaten to quit the program, leave the organization, tell off his boss, or miss a critical deadline.

The mentor's key task during this crucial phase, which may last for up to one year, is to demonstrate to the mentee that his terror is unfounded. This is done through symbolic enactments rather than verbal confrontations (which are relatively useless). The mentee is also encouraged to recall the origins of his terror in order to heal. The mentor then assists the mentee to face the part of himself that is actually dying. With this death, beliefs, relationships, and activities will be transformed. There is considerable education required to demonstrate that the need for attachment far surpasses the need for self-actualization. Learning this helps the mentee understand the purpose of his self-destructive impulses.

Finally, the mentor must keep the mentee on track to achieve his goals. This often involves a battle of wills in which the mentor proves to be a relentless slavedriver. In response, the mentee retaliates and succeeds; often in spite of himself. While he hates the mentor for driving him, he is quite thankful and amazed that the mentor has stoically prevailed. This phase involves daily phone contact to maintain the momentum for breakthrough.

This phase culminates in a transformation of self-love. The mentee, having projected both positive and hateful aspects of the self onto the mentor, claims his totality of being. Realizing that his own transformation has required steadfast support and total commitment, intimacy is also valued in a new way.

Having realized several of his 45 percent stretch goals, the mentee now profoundly understands the process of transformation.

Phase Five: Transformation (Transformation of Personal Freedom)

In the final interpersonal phase—transformation—the mentee is consciously in command of his considerable will. New challenges are eagerly and confidently sought. A longing to "repay" the mentor develops. As any attempt at reciprocity is frustrated (e.g., "If you care about me so much, then do the best you possibly can for X Corporation and your family."), the mentee is prodded toward becoming a corporate mentor in his own right.

During this launching phase, the mentor shifts into the role of mentoring supervisor and teaches the mentee the art of mentoring. Having experienced the process, as well as introjected the mentor's strengths, the mentee commits to mentor two organization members who are not direct reports. This phase takes between 6 and 12 months.

As "culture transformation" is viewed as a metaphor for the simultaneous transformation of a critical mass of executives through mentoring, it follows that systemic transformation will occur as mentoring unfolds. To ensure this, equal attention is paid to examining the impact of transformation on operational and leadership processes. As people transform, they seek to transform their business and environment. This alignment is the goal of culture transformation.

Whether you choose to adopt a highly structured and results-driven approach such as this; give participants free reign in designing a process; or arrive at some balance in between; you will need to document your approach and track results so that it can be delivered to executives within the same corporation in an organized way. Mentees frequently compare notes about their mentors and weekly mentoring experiences.

In the decade in which I have conducted, designed, and supervised CDM mentoring programs, I continue to feel great joy when witnessing their positive impact, whether through my own observations or our formal mentoring audit processes.

As a corporate therapist, you are uniquely trained to mentor executives through a self transformation that yields greater competitive advantage for their organizations.

In the next chapter, learn what executives say firsthand about their experience of being mentored by corporate therapists such as yourself.

14

Selling Mentoring Programs

Mentoring within the corporation has entered into a renaissance. The pace of change coupled with the requirement for greater flexibility and autonomy, have created the opportunity for mentoring to be viewed globally as a strategy for achieving a competitive advantage.

In selling prospective clients on the benefits of mentoring, a great deal of psychological education is required to explain the need, purpose, and underlying psychological processes and dynamics in play. While mentoring is currently in vogue, there is little sophistication in understanding the optimal approach to mentoring through utilizing psychologically-trained consultants.

To assist you, I have included the questions CEO's most frequently ask us when considering a corporate mentoring program along with our typical responses. Some CEOs see mentoring as part of their overall culture transformation strategy. Others view it as a tool for leadership development. Whatever the case, these questions and our answers will help you articulate the potential value of such a program.

What Are the Benefits of Mentoring?

The key benefit from mentoring that CEO's value most highly is the dramatic expansion of leadership behaviors and enhanced business results. Increases in sales, productivity and service and product quality are natural by-products of the mentoring process. Why such exceptional results? A well-structured mentoring relationship creates a solid source of confidential support and acceptance, so that the executive mentee is free to take risks, uncover operational deficits, and have the energy and insight to regularly identify and capture high-performance opportunities.

What Is the Difference Between Mentoring, Coaching, Counseling, and Managing? Aren't These All Buzz Words for What Executives Already Get Paid to Do?

Managing is making a professional commitment to developing a subordinate; coaching is a sporadic process to deal with performance problems; counseling is a process that helps deal with personal problems. The mentoring process differs from these in the nature of the relationship, the depth of the commitment and the level of skill required to actualize the inherent potential of the executive. Mentoring requires a deep commitment on the part of the mentor to see the mentee succeed, including a willingness to be available when needed, and use strategies and techniques that help the mentee accelerate his growth.

Shouldn't Mentoring Be an Informal Process?

No. When mentoring is done informally it can be destructive to both the mentee and corporation. Confidentiality is not monitored and corporate secrets can be leaked; the mentee's peers can sabotage his success through jealousy; opportunities for change and growth aren't properly recognized and leveraged; and personal disclosures can get the mentee into an embarrassing position, should the relationship fail. In addition, if the mentor and manager are of the opposite sex, and unaware of the dynamics of transference, boundaries can be crossed that may be detrimental for the corporation and personal lives of both parties. Mentoring is a powerful process and can be potentially dangerous if casually conducted.

How Are Candidates for Mentoring
Selected and Positioned?

Organizations review their management population to determine which candidates might have the greatest impact on achievement of the corporate vision and culture change; and which candidates should be groomed for greater responsibilities. For culture transformation, it is recommended that at least the top three management levels participate.

Do Mentors Give Input to
Performance Appraisals?

No. Mentoring is a confidential private experience that cannot legally be incorporated into corporate processes such as performance appraisals, succession planning, etc. Mentoring conducted by psychotherapists is governed by the APA Ethical Guidelines for Psychotherapists,[1] which outlines the mentee's right to confidentiality.

What Happens if a Mentor or Mentee
Leaves in Mid-Process?

On occasion, due to retirement or illness, a mentor or mentee may be unable to complete the full two-year process. In this event, a process is conducted which serves to bond the mentee to another mentor or optimally disengage from the relationship.

How Does Mentoring Impact
Succession Planning?

Executives involved in a mentoring program are in a far better position to determine who should succeed them in various positions as they retire or the organizational structure changes, as they are often more aware of the needs and demands of their role. Succession planning and mentoring can be linked, such that a pool of management talent is

---

[1] APA *Ethical Guildelines for Psychologists.* APA Publication, 1995.

constantly being developed and positioned, by providing mentoring to candidates being groomed for various promotions.

Isn't Teaching Psychological Techniques to Executives Dangerous?

In a management context, specific analytic and communication techniques adapted from various psychological change models can have a profound, positive effect on expanding an executive's contribution, building a quality consciousness in the organization and effecting quantum leaps in performance. Mentoring is not psychotherapy, which has as its context a personal, rather than professional, focus and purpose.

Doesn't the Mentor Get Emotionally Involved with the Mentee and Lose Objectivity or Get into Areas That Don't Concern Him?

No. The mentoring program is designed to provide each mentor with enough support and supervision so that objectivity and boundaries are carefully maintained. In addition, at six month intervals the program can be audited to determine client satisfaction. We find that mentoring is a powerfully rewarding and enriching experience for both mentees and mentors alike.

Does Mentoring Deal with Personal Problems, such as Alcoholism, Family Issues, and so on?

No. The focus of mentoring is restricted to professional development. Personal issues that may arise during mentoring are held in the strictest of confidence, and a referral is made for more personalized off-line EAP assistance, if needed.

How Do We Measure Results?

We suggest that the CEO and his executive team determine what qualitative and quantitative indicators can be monitored that will have the most direct impact on achieving the corporate vision, and that mentee participation be driven by measurable business performance goals. Indicators vary depending on the vision.

How Does Mentoring Work?

Mentoring works through these psychological processes that operate between the mentor and mentee:

- *Identification:* The establishment of compatibility and an intellectual bond.

- *Transference:* The development of an emotional bond with the mentor.

- *Introjection:* The natural and unconscious internalization of the mentor's skills and conscious awareness of the full range of the mentee's strengths.

- *Projection:* Utilizing strengths in a new way through expanding beliefs and values.

- *Generativity:* Fulfilling reciprocity needs by mentoring others.

In this role, mentors acting as growth agents, strategically further their mentee's progression into greater corporate success, and meet regressive needs to overcome defenses, fears, doubts, and other natural resistances to change. Once the mentoring process is complete, mentees become mentors within their own organization, thus expanding the mentoring culture.

What Is Self-Actualization?

Self-actualization is a structured process of facilitating the mentee into deeper levels of self discovery where true potentials lie. In most people, the basic self as the source of strengths, talents and will, is hidden behind layers of illusion, defense, conflict, and fear. By utilizing various analytic and communication techniques, the mentor and mentee determine how to best actualize the core self in the mentee, and what strategies will help him grow fastest.

Mentors are skilled in understanding the construction of the optimal leadership ego, and in developing two critical ego components necessary for ongoing transformation and competitive advantage: the *observing ego*, which allows the mentee to objectively examine his own behavior, and the *executive ego*, the part of the personality that consciously transforms perception and experience.

THE MENTORING AUDIT PROCESS

We at CDM conduct regular six-month audits of mentoring programs from confidential structured interviews with mentees. The following section summarizes the results of all of our audits taken between 1990 and 1995, involving over 20 large organizations. Corporate clients from many industries have benefited and been able to evaluate the impact of mentoring on their business.

Overall Audit Findings 1990–1995

1. Changes in Relationships after One Year of Mentoring
   - 60–75 percent of those audited typically report a significant positive change in their boss after one year of mentoring.
   - 50–65 percent report a positive shift in their relationship with their boss.
   - 75–90 percent report a major improvement in the quality of internal working relationships and morale of the organization.
   - 75–90 percent report both self and professional enhancement through improved relationships with colleagues, awareness of the vision, communication with teams, ability to facilitate culture change and reduced stress.
2. Impact on Teambuilding
   - 75–90 percent define themselves as growth agents for their staffs after one year of mentoring.
   - 75–80 percent define themselves as far more responsive to the needs of staff and sensitive to staff development.

- 65–75 percent of mentees report they are more organized, acknowledging, accessible, proactive, assertive and praising in relation to their direct reports.
- 70–85 percent of mentees report greater efficiency and productivity as a result of a major improvement in their team dynamic and relationship building skills.

3. Performance Turnarounds

- 70–80 percent of mentees report measurable performance breakthroughs of 30–45 percent within their first year of mentoring. These breakthroughs have been reported in:
    - departmental productivity
    - sales
    - bottomline contribution of their department (quartiled performance)
    - bottomline contribution to their region (ranked performance)
    - cross-selling ratio (products per customer)
    - sales productivity (revenue per salesperson)
    - sales efficiency (number of meetings to close sales)
    - service quality (mystery shopping indices)
    - reduction in processing errors
    - reduction in processing steps (streamlined operations)
- 10 percent of mentees report no significant differences in performance after one year, while 20 percent report measurable improvements in the 20–30 percent range.
    - These findings reflect a consistent trend in reported mentoring results over the last decade, in all organizations, which CDM has termed the 20-60-20 Rule:
    - 20 percent of mentees are natural champions who thrive on growth; therefore, they utilize mentoring to its maximum benefit;
    - 60 percent of mentees are open to facilitated growth and benefit tremendously from the mentoring technology within the 20–35 percent measurable performance improvement range.

- ○ 20 percent of mentees are generally growth-adverse, or uncomfortable with the intimacy and intensity of the mentoring relationship. These mentees tend to self-select out of the program, or are recommended to terminate the program on the advice of their mentor.

These results have been very effective in persuading a CEO to engage in a pilot program with us. You can point to our results as an example of the impact a mentoring program can have until you have generated your own track record.

15

Transforming Customers, Products, and Services

U ntil now, we have been focusing on transformation within the corporation in response to internal challenges. Yet, an equally powerful external force can impact its vision and direction. Customers collectively determine the organization's marketshare and dictate the trends of the marketplace. Organizations compete to predict customer trends in order to provide superior products and services. Market response time is crucial in ensuring competitive advantage.

Consumer behavior is shaped by social, economic, and political forces as well as by the products and services being consumed. As complex as it is to untangle the myriad factors that contribute to consumer's preferences, it is essential that organizations improve the ways they think about and study their customers. In our current times, markets and customers cannot be taken for granted.

There is much the corporate therapist can contribute to the process of understanding customers. In fact, customer analysis can be viewed as a psychotherapeutic process itself in that when customers abreact their experiences, they become more receptive to an organization's offering. Psychology is also extremely helpful in examining the decision-making processes customers use when choosing brands of products or services. It is a far more complex process than what it appears to the untrained nonclinical eye.

If you have expertise in object relations, you may find the process of customer decision making quite fascinating. If your expertise includes neurolinguistic programming, the gathering of consumer data and subsequent analysis and interpretation will be quite captivating. If you are a frustrated innovator, analyzing findings to create new products, services, and markets can be exhilarating.

As an example, CDM once retained Steve Lankton[1] to assist us in utilizing Eriksonian principles for a client's innovative television and print advertising campaign. As an expert in Eriksonian approaches to hypnosis, family therapy, and interface management, Lankton was encouraged to see the customer's viewpoint and then incorporate it into the design. The campaign was extremely successful in attracting attention and customers, and won several national awards. In the process, Steve became a trusted advisor to our CEO client in the utilization of Eriksonian principles for leadership.

In this chapter, we will examine current consulting processes for understanding customers and how a corporate therapist can provide a superior product offering. We will look at the forces shaping customer trends and how organizations have responded to changing consumer dynamics. Finally, we will look at a typical corporate dilemma to increase marketshare, and how CDM was able to help.

CUSTOMERS, VISIONS, AND CULTURE

Ideally, at the beginning of a culture transformation process, the CEO and his team will have studied the marketplace, the competition, and the anticipated changes in social, economic, and political forces as input for the corporate vision. As marketshare is based upon consumer acceptance and loyalty, it would appear that a comprehensive examination of the customer would be a priority. This activity however is often overlooked or downplayed. I have had CDM clients create products and services and then retain us to help them convince consumers to buy them! Or be halfway through a culture change when employees are still unaware of the psychology of their target markets.

The customer viewpoint as input to the corporate vision is obviously essential. It serves to focus the organization on meeting consumer needs. It provides an opportunity to discover avenues for competitive advantage. It can predict trends and develop future products and services. It can also inspire the culture toward embracing change as a means for survival. As a result of the power customers have in shaping

---

[1] Steve and Carol Lankton, *The Answer Within.* (New York: Brunner/Mazel, 1983).

the vision and culture, a sophisticated approach is needed to thoroughly understand their psychology.

While the need for specialized psychological expertise in examining consumer behavior and perception is enormous, for years organizations have relied mostly on market research to determine marketing strategy and product development. The quality of most qualitative market research is often considered poor, however.

Market researchers use a group interview format termed "focus groups." This methodology does not account for the ever-present dynamic of "groupthink," in which participants' needs for belonging and approval predominate over their willingness to disclose intimate beliefs essential to product/services design. Additionally, groups have a strong tendency to polarize into opposing views, leaving the critical "gray area" unexamined in the focus group format.

Market research interviewers are not trained to "listen with the third ear" and get beyond what the consumer is saying to what the deeper meaning, belief, or perception is. Therefore, their interpretation of data is often superficial. Interviewing at the deeper levels of the inner self requires the strategic use of language, as well as psychological techniques including mirroring, regressing, and joining. Market researchers are not trained in establishing the "transferential" bond required to obtain access to these deeper levels.

Market researchers are not trained psychological clinicians, therefore they are unskilled in managing the dynamics of the "inner self" which is the source of decision-making. Typical questionnaires and processes access the level of consciousness of "illusion" rather than "will" where gestalts and beliefs are formed.

Finally, the examination of the unconscious terrain of symbols, sensations, memories, and feelings, as well as the interpretation required, demands a sophisticated analytic approach. Clinicians are best equipped to identify hidden connections, unifying threads, and specific themes. These can then be translated into service/product designs that ensure competitive advantage, as well as a strategy for mobilizing loyalty contracts with current and prospective customers.

Typically, a corporate marketing department contracts with a market research firm to examine the feasibility or potential of a product, service, or target group. A study is conducted and a report is furnished to the authorizing client (typically, the marketing director). He or she then reviews the implications of the findings with colleagues and the chief executive's senior team. Recommendations are integrated into the strategic direction of the organization. As you can see from this process, data can be interpreted several times, thus diluted.

Often, the psychology of various target groups is not closely examined to understand the myriad factors that contribute to the perception of a product or service. Take a CDM example: It was found that professional women as a target market typically shy away from seeking financial advice. A market research firm recommended specific changes to the advertising approach as a result of this finding. When CDM looked at the same data, we discovered an underlying conflict that women face when attempting to accumulate wealth. The real issue was their changing perception of themselves as they earned more money. We then incorporated this dynamic into a financial advisory interview process. The targeted female could now abreact her feelings, and in the process, build a trusting bond with the advisor. Through this profound experience, she was able to transcend the conflict by articulating it. This led to a higher perceived value of the service by the female consumer. Advertising the service focused on positioning women as deserving of wealth.

Another example of the simplistic approach to customer psychology that successful organizations routinely take is Coca Cola's change in formula.

When Coca Cola changed the recipe for the soft drink to which generations of people the world over have been devoted, we ended up back with the original renamed "Classic Coke" in response to an uproar from customers. The change shook customer loyalty and was enough to cause a reversal of strategy.

This expensive embarrassment probably could have been avoided if Coca Cola had understood that customers make product decisions at an emotional level. Their decision-making process is largely unconscious and based on object relations. For example, if you have grown up in a family that drinks Coca Cola instead of Pepsi, by the time you are an adolescent, you will have a primary identification with Coca Cola. "Coke" is incorporated into your object world. If Coca Cola changes its formula, you feel personally betrayed and unsettled.

I offer a similar example of how useful psychology might have been in ensuring a different kind of competitive advantage.

Two international airlines attempted to improve their service offering to business travelers. Both had since accepted that as a result of frequent flyer programs, most first-class seats go to upgraded business class ticket holders. Yet, the business traveler is still the most desirable customer that an airline can rely upon. Unbeknownst to the other, each airline repackaged their first class service to rival the current industry standard.

One airline chose to eliminate their first class cabin altogether. Their concept was to offer all business class customers the finer aspects of first class service. Toward that end, seats were enlarged, the menu was improved, the wine list upgraded, and personalized videotape players were provided at each seat. While these tactics worked to increase sales following the airlines promotion of the service, customer feedback was generally uninspiring.

By contrast, the other airline conducted a comprehensive psychological analysis into the deeper needs that customers have for flying first class. While food, comfort, and entertainment were superficially important, the deeper longing that customers have is to get some sleep! To acknowledge this, the airline redesigned every aspect of its first-class service to extend and enhance sleeping.

Rather than the usual two hours of waiting for dinner to be served, they introduced a hot/cold buffet shortly after take-off. The customer was provided with a pajama-like sweat suit and given a fluffy goose-down comforter and king-size pillow. Cabin lights were quickly dimmed. Video selections were made prior to boarding. Breakfast was served 30 minutes before the actual descent began.

Customers immediately loved this service and enthusiastic word of mouth made it an overnight sensation. The airline increased its paid first-class revenues. It has since gone on to experiment with actual pull-out beds on board with full customer support.

While the first airline made an attempt at differentiating its service, it did not look deeply enough at the nonverbal symbols that customers unconsciously associate with perceived superior service. For example, the blankets were threadbare; many of the video players malfunctioned; and the staff behaved as though their customers should be grateful for whatever they provided (as they didn't deserve to be in first class anyway). It became obvious to customers that the airline was not truly committed to delivering a first class service to customers who only paid business class fares. If it were, each symbol of service excellence would be included and integrated into a seamless delivery.

While both airlines benefited from meeting customer needs better, the sleep-sensitive service created a new standard of customer service for the industry. All first class services will be perceived now to be lacking if there are not beds on board. This kind of competitive advantage is a powerful weapon in retaining and attracting customers, thus increasing marketshare.

This dynamic is extremely relevant to our times, based upon how consumers are now choosing brands, services, and products. There are currently three social trends greatly influencing consumer dynamics and psychology.

SOCIAL TRENDS INFLUENCING
CONSUMER PSYCHOLOGY

The first social trend is the breakdown of the American family system, evidenced by the average divorce rate of over 50 percent. Additionally, merger and acquisition activity in the United States has quadrupled since 1970, creating a situation in which many Americans are losing their at-home and corporate families simultaneously, creating emotional stress, health problems, and decreased work performance. This trend has created a great need for emotional support to fill the void. As a result, many Americans unconsciously look to relationships with providers of products and service deliverers to provide constancy, advice, and direction. Organizations who keenly understand this dynamic and know how to present themselves as extended family members, strategically fulfilling emotional as well as other needs, are succeeding brilliantly at life-cycle selling and customer retention. In light of this trend, the perceived quality and depth of the customer relationship is a competitive advantage.

Second, America is selling to the "Me Generation." As the children of depression-era parents, they are enjoying social freedoms more expansively than any other generation in American history, and with dizzying effects. The "Age of Narcissism" is challenging organizations to upgrade in every conceivable way. As employees, baby boomers are far less likely to work two decades to earn an executive management position or to remain loyal during slow markets. In order to protect their customer base, top organizations are scrambling to provide incentives and mentoring programs to retain superior staff. As consumers, baby boomers are demanding, impatient, eager to criticize, and fickle toward any one institution. Striking the right balance between catering to target markets while providing products for mass appeal, is a competitive advantage.

The third social trend has the power to transform every dimension of American life, yet its true significance is not fully appreciated.

Taken together, technological advances and international competition have quickened the pace of American life—leading to a growing national demand for speed, choice, and convenience. For the right-handed, left-brain dominant, analytically-oriented American, life is literally moving faster than his ability to assimilate it. (In fact, cognitive studies have demonstrated that the human memory limit is seven unrelated items, plus or minus two, before a breakdown in learning occurs and alternate channels for information processing must be accessed). In this information overload era, innovative advertisers are shifting their message to appeal to the emotional, intuitive, associative, "unconscious" right half of the brain, which processes information at a significantly faster rate. This shift to right-brain thinking is changing how Americans form perceptions and make buying decisions. "Gut feeling" and "intuition" are replacing competitive analysis and rate shopping.

When perception is largely comprised of emotional factors, the need to understand how customers form associations and identify with products, services, and providers is of paramount importance. The interpersonal skills and strategies required to create customer feelings of loyalty, sponsorship, and reciprocity are a competitive advantage.

Given these social trends: elegance in packaging, a broad product offering, an exciting selling environment, speed in delivery, and a sales and service style based on nurturance and empathy offer enormous opportunities for progressive organizations.

THE CORPORATE THERAPIST AS CUSTOMER ANALYST

As a corporate therapist, you can capitalize on the need organizations have to better understand and care for their customers. In fact, you can design a full service for improving the customer relationship; from understanding target markets to incorporating the customer viewpoint into an overall culture change strategy.

A comprehensive customer program should contain three phases: a psychological study of the customer in each target segment; feedback of research findings to management and employees through a comprehensive training program that is based on the results of the customer study; and feedback to the customer on an ongoing basis regarding the organization's progress and performance. You can elect to offer a full service, or just specialize in a particular aspect of customer analysis, such as making the initial video of findings after interviewing is completed.

CDM's customer analysis process was designed after observing a badly conducted market research study. Jennifer Buton Tallow and I were on a CDM assignment to an organization that had retained a qualitative market research firm to study its customers preferences.

We sat behind a one-way mirror in the interviewing facility. We quickly found that we had to stifle our groans, when we saw how inappropriately and naively psychological techniques were being applied by an interviewer without psychological training or skills. Guided imagery, regression, and several Eriksonian techniques were poorly attempted. The customer, trying to cooperate, was embarrassed and confused. We, as observers, were appalled. So we decided to create our own CDM customer analysis process to protect future clients from such a comedy of errors again!

Not all market research processes are ineffective. However, most traditional approaches do not presently contain the psychological technologies to gain access to the deeper decision-making process inherent in the right brain mode. The roots of these technologies are found in the clinical disciplines of psychology. They include:

- ○ *Neurospsychology:* The study of the brain and behavior;

- ○ *Psychoanalysis:* Accessing the deepest self where belief structures, patterns of behavior and identification and introjection of objects are formed and maintained;

- ○ *Neurolinguistic programming:* The strategic use of language and suggestion to influence perception and behavior;

- ○ *Therapeutic interviewing:* The development of a trusting therapeutic bond ("transference") in which profound insights can be accessed and candidly shared.

CDM designed its Customer Analysis to meet the need global competitors have for understanding how to best build and maintain customer loyalty and referrals, as well as to design products and services that are breakthroughs. "Breakthroughs" condition a new generation of customers toward higher satisfaction and expectations, therefore increasing competitive advantage.

The CDM process is designed to encourage introspection and insight (Figure 15.1). These processes lead to clarity for the customer as

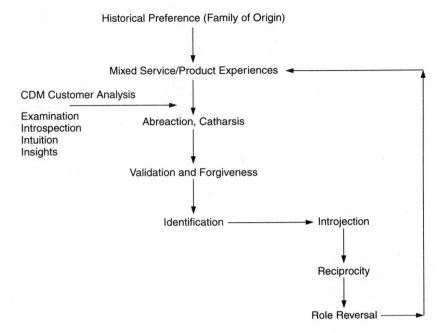

Figure 15.1 Creating/Building Loyal Customer Psychology.

well as the clinician, as to what beliefs, symbols, and feelings create the dynamics of loyalty and reciprocity. We also examine what symbols would mobilize these dynamics in a new product or service offering. A thorough understanding and integration of beliefs is achieved. When opinions and thresholds of acceptability are researched, the deeper issues that bridge the gap from acceptability to loyalty and reciprocity are discovered.

Through the use of trained clinicians who are "architects of the unconscious," our process incorporates deep relaxation, intimate bonding, guided imagery, free association, and an extensive examination of historical influences and symbolic triggers. Particular attention is paid to the processes of abreaction and catharsis. Disappointments in products and service providers are explored. A relational sales strategy for overcoming service or delivery barriers is designed to help implement a loyal customer culture.

Customers enjoy the process, citing its benefits as stress reduction and a method for accessing and validating their inner selves. A secondary gain to our corporate clients is the promotional benefits of the

174 / From Couch to Corporation

service. Customers feel special when included in the organization's strategy and planning process. Often CEOs create a Customer Advisory Board and continue to meet with research participants quarterly for ongoing feedback.

The outcome of the CDM Customer Analysis is a video that illustrates the full spectrum of perceptions and ideas that customers shared. These films have proven to be a powerful medium for customers to speak directly to the CEO and senior executives without interpretations or filters. Further, they are the educational foundation for subsequent customer relationship training. The salesforce is trained in a more effective and efficient sales process, based on findings. Customer satisfaction measures and tools are created as well.

We carefully detail differences in the psychology of the ambivalent ("typical") customer as well as the loyal one. Notably, a loyal customer identifies deeply with the product, service, and organization, thus introjects it into their intimate life—and becomes dependent on it. Products that are introjected are incorporated into one's personal sense of identity ("my favorite airline," the "car I drive," "our pizza place") and fiercely defended.

Therefore, when inevitable disappointments occur due to inconsistencies, rationalizations are automatically created in the customer's mind in order to protect the introject. Fluctuations in price, convenience, and competitive offerings are dismissed. In a psychological "role reversal" customers will mobilize their personal networks to help out an organization with whom they identify. In this instance, they elect to support the organization through tough times.

In many cases, ad campaigns will strike an emotional chord in resonating with customers deepest beliefs ("Just Do It"—NIKE). Reframing a familiar and trusted provider ("Solutions for a Small Planet"—IBM) into something exciting, fun, and different catches customers by surprise. They often will react by internalizing both the message and the organization, then promote it throughout their network.

Conversely, an unbonded customer will grow increasingly frustrated with adequate or poor service/product quality. This silent apathy will build and culminate in a total rejection of both the organization and its products/services when the final insult is felt. Without abreaction of their disappointment, they will disparage the product or service to the marketplace, ensuring potential customers stay away.

For example, medical malpractice lawsuits are often a result of long-term frustration with many doctors, even though the last one is sued. CDM has designed an abreaction process for the healthcare industry in which patients are encouraged to vent their frustration at treatment they have received from previous service providers, to reduce the likelihood of undeserved malpractice claims against the current provider. Figures 15.1 and 15.2 look at the psychodynamics of loyal versus unhappy customers and their impact on marketshare.

For example, in our work with financial service customers globally, we have found that the corporate vision must start with understanding

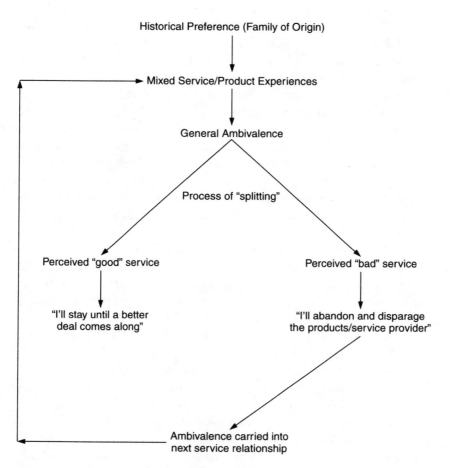

Figure 15.2   Typical Customer Psychology.

..omer's vision for "perfect" service. This includes customers perceived needs and interests, previous history with other financial services organizations, their vision for the perfect delivery vehicle and service process, and how they make decisions in selecting an institution.

We have found that customers have a hostile-dependent relationship to financial services institutions. They feel toward them much the way they feel toward the Internal Revenue Service (a necessary evil). They believe that while bankers are the most trustworthy, financial service providers are typically uninformed, indifferent, and more concerned with collecting money than meeting customer's needs.

Customers strongly associate self-worth with net worth, and have many financial services relationships to protect their privacy. Embarrassed at how poorly they manage their financial options and responsibilities, many people rely on friends and relatives for financial advice. People who earn significantly more money than their parents are also conflicted about wealth, therefore manage it poorly.

Errors in mailings and account statements, uncaring and poorly trained employees, and long waits for service outrage customers. Customers' vision of a perfect financial services institution is one in which the employees care about them personally, actively encourage and support their financial growth; educate them about financial strategies and options; and are accountable and apologetic about service errors. Further, customers believe that interest rates are less important than the services that are provided.

In our studies, findings such as these are then compared to the institution's current functioning. Major changes in organizational culture, structure, marketing strategy, product mix, systems, recruiting, compensation, and physical layout are considered. Particular emphasis is given to those aspects of the service that have deep meaning to the customer in determining the credibility and likability of the institution. We have found, for instance, that an untidy work station or ATM area, an employee who avoids eye contact, a bored voice on the phone, and interruptions during a sales or service process represent particularly upsetting symbols to financial services customers.

Further, the typical customer analysis would include a thorough understanding of the emotional needs of each target segment throughout the life cycle, so that marketing or sales processes can be refined to lead to rapid unconflicted buying decisions. For example, we have found that the elderly often have hidden sources of funds, enjoy seminars for social value, require a family-like relationship in order to do business, and are eager to support the younger service provider by offering leads and referrals.

The final step we would consider is how to redesign the sales process in order to capitalize on these psychological opportunities. In the above market, a leveraged sales strategy might include a relationship with the director of an elderly social group, delivering a curriculum of breakfast seminars, personally interviewing the wealthiest members about their parenting years, and what financial advice they have for the current generation. These activities can be the foundation for the future selling of the target market on the benefits of the institution and in asking for sponsorship and referrals.

Customer analysis findings are then incorporated into a comprehensive training program that would include a thorough analysis of implications for all organizational levels, the psychology of each market segment and the interpersonal skills, precise narratives and process steps for selling each market segment. The program would examine what negative associations exist, then provide precise narratives for transforming them. It would detail how each level of the organization is perceived by customers, and is responsible for symbolizing superior service. It would describe how expectations for service will be measured at each level and how frequently. Most importantly, it would define what each organizational level and functional group needs from each other to perform internally at a level of zero-error service.

These studies have led to major breakthroughs in competitive advantage. For example, as a result of our customer analysis process in banks, we were able to create an interview product which we named the Financial Vision Interview. It is a three-interview process in which customers explore beliefs about money and create a vision for personal wealth. As a result, typically two-thirds of customers who engage in the process are receptive to doing more business with their bank through closing competitors accounts and transferring assets. This led to consistently doubling or tripling the cross selling ratio, that is, the number of products and services that each customer has with the bank. The more products and services, the more profit for the institution.

As a result, CDM is sought after by major financial institutions globally who want to achieve a breakthrough in cross-selling. We have since implemented customer programs in Canada, France, Spain, Amsterdam, England, Scotland, Germany, Switzerland, as well as Malaysia and Australia. Many of these have led to long-term culture transformation projects as well. So you can see how powerful a clinical eye can be in detecting an unrecognized need in the marketplace.

To conduct your own customer analysis, start by interviewing the CEO and senior executives to determine how much they currently know about their customers. Review their current file of market research. Understand the overall strategic plan to see where new products fit in. Find an opportunity in which the psychological perspective would be valuable. Pose a series of questions that can be best addressed from a psychological perspective.

Your client will want to determine the sample size and selection criteria. You can contact a local market research firm to help obtain participants and provide a facility for interviewing and videotaping customers. It can be very powerful to make a short video (30 minutes) of key quotes that highlight general as well as unusual perspectives.

Your recommendations for changes in products, advertising, packaging, promotion, and selling will come from your interview data. Be sure to include recommendations for training the personnel who relate to customers in your findings.

Selling customer studies is not as difficult as selling either wall-to-wall culture transformation or mentoring programs. Simply going to a place where customers are and videotaping their reactions to various products and services can be enough to generate corporate interest.

Think about those products and services that you use and how they could be improved. Then approach the provider with an idea for a study. At CDM, we have attracted several large studies using this simple method. Studying products that you use provides you with a headstart in both experience and insight.

You can also contact advertising agencies who typically represent major corporate clients. They are often quite receptive to new approaches that can help crystallize a creative campaign. In this approach, you will be a subcontractor to a creative team.

A typical customer project takes between six weeks and three months to deliver. This includes production time and a final presentation of findings. A typical sample size is between 50 and 100 customers.

These studies can be helpful during your transition from couch to corporation, as they require a short- versus long-term commitment. They also provide an excellent medium for leveraging your clinical skills.

PART FOUR

Your Competitive Advantage in Corporate Therapy

16

Leaving Your Legacy Behind

The role of corporate therapist is a powerful, visible one. Therefore, you want to give considerable thought as to how you will define it for yourself. Since many of the rules, boundaries, and conditions for psychotherapy do not apply, there is an opportunity to creatively design how you will operate; and to some extent, how you will be perceived by your clients.

All consulting engagements eventually end. Often what begins as a brief study develops into a multiyear project. However, at the appropriate juncture, your involvement will be terminated. How do you want to be remembered? What role will you play, if any, after your work is done?

Having pondered these questions for 15 years privately and with various clinical supervisors, I have arrived at my own definition of the corporate therapist role. It is in response to what clients have needed over the years, and my own experiences as a corporate therapist.

To me, the role provides the opportunity for client self-examination that psychotherapy offers within the context of a highly strategic approach to transformation. While there are interventions at multiple levels within the corporation, loyalty to the CEO client must come first. This does not mean confidences should be betrayed. However, when a conflict in interest arises, the CEO's needs and priorities take precedence. I have attempted to clarify this as much as possible in the CDM Confidentiality Contract that clients sign.

While the corporation pays for CDM's services, the CEO's personal development and well-being are critical. Toward that end, equal (or greater) time is spent on his intrapsychic dynamics and barriers. Once explored in depth, it is essential that they then be examined in relation to his organization and family. The more self-awareness he has, the better he will lead. The better his marriage functions, the better he will perform. While I do not often see his wife at his office, the organization is usually aware that we are working together. This has a positive liberating effect on the culture.

Although his children have been greatly affected by his career and often require support, I function more as their mentor than therapist. While we may have several sessions early in the project to characterize relationships within the family from a multi-generational perspective; I have found there is not enough time to devote to the children's issues. While I maintain a therapeutic role with the couple, I refer the children for outside treatment.

I am, however, available for special projects at the children's request. These have included help with college and graduate school applications, job searches and recommendations, surprise birthday and anniversary parties, and premarital screening and counseling.

I also interview as many "significant others" as required. These have included siblings, parents, grandparents, board directors, friends, family doctors, personal trainers and sports coaches. Since CDM's approach is so encompassing, I feel the need to gather voluminous data in order to see the picture separate from what the CEO perceives. Some of my most critical insights have come from interviewing a child, parent or long-time friend. As I approach this journey like a detective searching for clues, there must be permission given by the client to pursue all possible "leads."

One of my clinical supervisors empowered me by exclaiming, "You know, the whole world is now your office." Another characterized my role as, "Have psychology, will travel." Since then, I meet with clients wherever it is timely: in their office in the wee morning hours, over dinner at the country club, on the corporate jet, at their home on Sunday mornings, on the ski slopes in Vail (where we live in the winter), at the track while we run together, or at some midpoint between the United States and their home base on another continent. I try to include their wives in as many meetings as possible. Some attend virtually every session. Others come as often as their work schedule permits. When they can't attend, we summarize the meeting by phone.

Clients and their wives often visit with my husband and me during projects and after they are over. If we are currently working together, they stay at a hotel. After disengagement, they often stay at our homes or we at theirs. Quite different from psychotherapy, the mentor is viewed as an extended family member. Former clients have taken vacations with us, sailing, rafting, hiking, camping, and scuba diving. After a program is over, this is an excellent way to get caught up with the progress the organization has made since my absence.

When a former CEO client decides to leave his organization, I am usually contacted for strategic input and emotional support. When a significant other dies or marries, I am included in the rituals. I receive gifts, cards, and letters for many years after a program is completed. The bond may change form, but we remain eternally connected.

This role, as I've defined it, requires discipline and careful boundary management. For example, after a project formally ends, I do not accept more fees. I believe that, by definition, I am available upon demand for life, much like an older parent. Further, while my life is open to observation, I do not disclose much about myself. On social occasions, I insist that the focus remain on the client, much like a parent does when on a family vacation with grown children. Except for occasional references, I do not ask for or expect anything from my clients once our work is done.

While this policy has proven challenging, I believe it serves the needs of the client. For example, years after a project ended, I was asked to facilitate a CEO's divorce. Another time, I helped a former client cope with the death of a child. During these times, I witnessed profound healing and no money changed hands. Clients believe that I really care about them when a relationship is tested in this way. As one wryly put it, "Well, I don't know why, but you are still a part of us, and you're always invited to weddings and funerals."

As a result of the role that I have defined, client relationships are intense, profound, and dramatic. As they are confrontational by design, they evolve into deep connections. However, within the context of culture transformation in which every minute counts, it seems essential to be this involved. There might be contact several times a day, including most vacations and evenings. To manage this workload, CDM's policy is to engage in only four large projects at one time.

For quality control and technical assistance, I receive two hours of individual supervision a week either in person or over the phone. As I am expected to be available upon demand, I ask that my supervisor do the same. Typically, we negotiate an annual retainer paid monthly to compensate for unscheduled phone calls and strategy sessions. In addition to reviewing my assessment and approach, we engage often in "micro-transactional analysis" in which I replay a dialogue and we critique its effectiveness. We then role-play several therapeutic options. Supervisors have included family therapists, psychoanalysts, behaviorists, neuropsychologists, and specialists in group dynamics, gestalt, psychodrama, sex therapy, and cognitive therapy, among others.

My own approach has been effective. Our projects end well and clients remain positive references and extended family friends. With supervision and a supportive network of friends and family, I have been able to manage the demands of the role. Obviously, the years when I was single dictated a different set of boundaries!

Without a large support system, I believe the corporate therapist can be in major danger. Corporate clients, in their quest for idealization, will attempt to lure you into areas where you do not belong. They may expect you to advise them on business issues in which you have no expertise. They may attempt to make you a "friend" in order to deflect their anxieties about power or engulfment. If you are single, there can be fantasies of a romance. If you are going through your own growing pains, you can be susceptible to an unproductive countertransference.

While my own supervisors have not been corporate therapists, they have been invaluable in helping me often examine the implications of my role. They have also been frank in assessing my skills and capability for undertaking a particular case. More than once, I've turned work down because we agreed I was not mature nor skillful enough to optimally deliver what was needed.

In defining your own role, start by asking yourself what legacy you want to leave behind? How do you want your clients to remember you? Are you comfortable seeing yourself as a life-transforming agent? Or is it better for you to limit your role to being a corporate coach?

Unlike practicing psychotherapy, there are no rules for defining your consultancy practice. While you still follow ethical guidelines, the corporate context requires that you also examine how to serve your clients in this new role. The more consciously you do this, the clearer your actions will be perceived.

It is extremely rewarding to play a significant role in the life of a CEO and his extended at-home and organizational family. You can make this role work for both the client and yourself, once you examine several factors that come into play.

YOUR "SELF" IS THE PRIMARY GROWTH AGENT

My training and supervision in Comprehensive Family Therapy (CFT) demonstrated that as a change agent and healer, there is quite literally no place to hide. Therefore, it is the responsibility of the corporate therapist to "heal thyself" in order to earn the right to heal others. This may require extensive self-growth work to achieve full awareness of your dynamics and unique gifts. Once you claim your totality, you can design various strategies to compensate for your deficits as well as leverage your strengths.

ARE YOU TOUGH ENOUGH
FOR TRANSMUTATION?

Transformation requires that the mentee grows strong enough to confront his shame and self-hatred. Initially, this is projected onto the corporate therapist, as hatred and rage are part of the mentoring dance. In addition, terrors of abandonment, engulfment, entrapment, rejection, and annihilation are enacted. This phase tests the corporate therapist's mettle and commitment. Negative transference may last several months.

To be effective, you must frankly confront your projections and weaknesses. The support of a supervisor is essential to remain impermeable to client attacks. While transmutation episodes are excellent opportunities for healing your client, there are correct and incorrect responses. Without practicing them in supervision first, the chance to help the client transform can be lost.

WHEN TO LET GO?

If you have chosen to mentor your corporate clients, you will have made a deep commitment to a long-term process. Sacrifices will be made over time. You may cancel a vacation; you might decide to receive therapy to transmute a barrier. With all this investment comes attachment. As a result, your clients trust you when you propose more work. Yet, at some point, it will become apparent that it is time for you to move on. Will you be tuned in to these signals? Or have you become too attached to let go?

I strongly advise that you define a clear endpoint to your consulting process to protect yourself and your client from over-dependence. I have been called upon too many times to help guilty CEO's politely disengage from dependent consultants who have fallen into the trap of "living off the fat of the land." The truth is, most consultants never want to let go, as the consulting industry functions on the concept of extension. As a corporate therapist, you cannot afford to be included in this unrespected camp. Even if long-term, your role must sooner or later end.

Mentee clients signal you when launching is imminent. They appear more self-assured and less willing to give you airtime. As a role model for correct rapprochement, you have strived to progress them into higher levels of mastery and new arenas. Once they have received what they need from you and are grounded in other relationships, your role and its importance will naturally wane.

It is helpful to deal with the impending loss of the client relationship in your own supervision. Abreacting your feelings about the client and the role you have played both integrates learning as well as helps you separate. For me, having a long-term client "grow up" often triggered abandonment fears. To manage these, I made it a rule to have only infrequent phone contact basis with a terminated client throughout the first year of "launching." Only after this separation could I be confident I was acting in his, rather than my own, best interest.

I share my own experiences in the hope that you can avoid some of the pitfalls inherent in this unusual context. After you have completed your first long-term project, you will be able to review the implications of your defined role, and adjust it accordingly.

Just remember that like a psychotherapist, a corporate therapist will be internalized and remembered later as a highly significant figure. It is crucial that you understand the full impact of your role before you engage in it. Your legacy will affect the organization's ability to seek helpers long into the future.

17

Taking Care
of Yourself

As psychotherapists are natural healers, they tend to be quite generous by nature. However, even those who have worked through hidden agendas as to why they have become therapists are often neglectful of their God-given narcissistic rights! It is essential to be extremely self-loving as a corporate therapist. The more abundant that you feel, the more energy that you will have to give.

At one time, I was rather withholding when it came to nurturing and rewarding myself. However, I realized that my new role demanded a certain parity with chief executives in order to be viewed as a powerful figure. I then recognized that taking care of myself was a business priority. This made honoring my own narcissistic longings more acceptable.

I urge you too to seriously consider the toll that practicing corporate therapy will take on your time and energy. Protect yourself by making the commitment to take superior care of yourself. The better that you cope with your own needs for regression and refueling, the more powerful your progressive thrusts will be.

EXTEND YOUR LIFE

A corporate therapy practice is stressful and physically demanding. Long hours, frequent travel and highly active sessions are the norm. To protect your health, assess your predisposition to various illnesses upfront. Be proactive in designing a life extension program in which both the quality and duration of your life is expanded. Vitamins and various other supplements can make a major difference in your overall cognitive abilities and general emotional functioning.

REWARD YOURSELF

The financial impact that you can have on an organization in which you have helped the chief executive transform himself is literally worth millions. Spend a portion of your fees on rewarding yourself with vacations, gifts, and financial security. The less needy that you are, the more objective and powerful you will be in confronting growth barriers within your clients. You need to always come from a position of fulfillment and well-being in order to be effective.

EXAMINE YOUR PURPOSE AS A PART OF THE UNIVERSAL PLAN

Meditation, whether done as a formal ritual or as daily prayer and contemplation, is essential in unburdening yourself of those influences that distract you from your work. Since corporate therapy is a powerful role, it is quite useful to ask yourself; "What is my ultimate purpose in the life of this client? How can I do what is required in an optimal way?"

If you examine these issues daily, you may be amazed at the guidance and support that the universe will provide to you. This process helps to align you naturally with the universal laws.[1] As you internalize them, they become a driving force in your corporate therapy work. In time, you'll feel a part of the universal plan as your practice continues to unfold.

DEMAND AND RECEIVE SUPPORT

As a giver of energy and emotional support, you have earned the right to receive it as well. Examine your relationships to assess whether they

---

[1] Deepak Chopra, *The Way of the Wizard: Twenty Spiritual Lessons for Creating the Life You Want*. (New York: Crown Publishers, 1996).

provide the nurturing and support that you deserve. Particularly, your significant other must be aware of how to regress and refuel you in a transformational way.

There is no room for masochism and martyrdom in the life of the corporate therapist. You must be an inspiration and model of health and happiness for others. Your friends and family can keep you grounded and energized, once you teach them how.

The corporate world is becoming increasingly demanding while, as a society, we are providing fewer support systems and benefits. If having read this book, you are inspired to transist into consulting within the corporate setting, the opportunity for you to flourish is currently there.

FOR MORE INFORMATION

CDM Inc., offers videos, weekend workshops, and intensive training for clinicians making the transition from couch to corporation. Continuing education credits are given for program attendance. Subcontractors must be corporate therapy seminar graduates.

For information on CDM programs and services, contact corporate headquarters at:

Creative Dimensions in Management, Inc.
Lee Park, Main Building
Suite 200
1100 East Hector Street
Conshohocken, PA 19428
Phone: 610/825-8350
Fax: 610/825-8354
http://www.corpmentoring.com
e-mail address: cdm at corpmentoring.com

BIBLIOGRAPHY

Balient, M., *The Basic Fault. Therapeutic Aspects of Regression*, Brunner/Mazel, New York, 1969.

Bateson, G., *Steps to an Ecology of Mind*, Chandler Publishing, New York, 1972.

Beck, A., *Cognitive Therapy and Emotional Disorder*, International University Press, New York, 1976.

Bennis, W., *On Becoming a Leader*, Addison Wesley, Lexington, MA, 1994.

Bennis, W., & Townsend, R., *Reinventing Leadership: Strategies to Empower the Organization*, William Morrow, New York, 1995.

Board, R., *The Psychoanalysis of Organizations: A Psychoanalytic Approach to Behavior in Groups and Organizations*, Routledge, London, 1978.

Bowlby, J., *Attachment and Loss*, Basic Books, New York, 1969.

Bowlby, J., *Separation*, Basic Books, New York, 1973.

Brown, J., *The Social Psychology of Industry*, Penguin Books, New York, 1954.

Burne M.D., E., *The Structure and Dynamics of Organizations and Groups*, Grove Press, Inc., New York, 1963.

Burrough, B., & Helyar, J., *Barbarians at the Gate: The Fall of R.J.R. Nabisco*, Harper & Row, New York, 1991.

Campbell, Ed, E., *Man and Transformation*, Princeton/Bollinger, Princeton, NJ, 1964.

Champy, J., *Re-engineering Management*, HarperCollins, New York, 1994.

Champy, J., & Hammer, J., *Re-engineering Corporations*, HarperCollins, New York, 1994.

Charney, I., *Existential/Dialectical Marital Therapy: Breaking the Secret Code of Marriage*, Brunner/Mazel, New York, 1990.

Coleman, A., & Bexton, W., (Eds.), *Group Relations Reader*, Grex, California, 1975.

Cosement, P., *On Learning from the Patient*, Tavistock/Routledge, London, 1985.

Erikson, E., *Childhood and Society*, W.W. Norton, New York, 1950.

Fairbairn, W. R. D., *An Objects Relations Theory of the Personality*,

Fritz, R., *The Path of Least Resistance*, Halliday, Boston, MA, 1984.

Gibbard, G., & Hartman, J., (Eds.), *Analysis of Groups*, Jossey-Bass, New York, 1974.

Guerin, P., *Family Therapy: Therapy and Practice*, Gardner Press, New York, 1976.

Guntrip, H., *Schizoid Phenomena, Object Relations and the Self*, International University Press, New York, 1969.

Hatcher, C., & Himeslstein, D., (Eds.), *The Handbook of Gestalt Therapy*, J. Aronson, New York, 1976.

Henry, J., *Pathways to Madness*, Random House, New York, 1965.

Hickman, G., & Silva, M., *Creating Excellence*, New American Library, New York, 1984.

Hilgard, E., *The Experience of Hypnosis*, Harcourt Brace Jovanovich, Orlando, FL, 1965.

Jung, C., *The Psychology of Transference*, Bollinger/Princeton, Princeton, NJ, 1966.

Kantor, D., & Lehr, W., *Inside the Family: Toward a Theory of Family Process*, Harper Colophon Books, New York, 1976.

Kantor, D., & Rosebeth, D., *Men and Women of the Corporation*, Harper Colophon Books, New York, 1979.

Kepner, C., & Trego, B., *The New Rational Manager*, Princeton Research Press, Princeton, NJ, 1981.

Kirschner, D., & Kirschner, S., *Comprehensive Family Therapy: An Integration of Systemic and Psychodynamic Treatment Models*, Brunner/Mazel, New York, 1986.

Kirschner, D., & Kirschner, S., *Comprehensive Therapy of Couples and Families*, John Wiley, New York, 1996.

Kirschner, D., Kirschner, S., & Rappaport, R., *Working with Adult Incest Survivors*, Brunner/Mazel, New York, 1993.

Klein, M., *Envy and Gratitude and Other Works, 1946–1963*, Delacorte Press, London, 1975.

Lankton, C., & Lankton, S., *Tales of Enchantment*, Brunner/Mazel, New York, 1989.

Lankton, S., & Lankton, C., *The Answer Within: A Clinical Framework of Eriksonian Hypnotherapy*, Brunner/Mazel, New York, 1983.

Levinson, H., *The Exceptional Executive: A Psychological Conception*, New American Library, New York, 1968.

Levinson, H., *Psychological Man*, Levinson Institute, Boston, MA, 1976.

Levinson, H., & Rosenthal, S., *CEO: Corporate Leadership in Action*, Basic Books, New York, 1984.

Lewis, R., & Walker, B., *Why Should White Guys Have All the Fun?*, John Wiley, New York, 1995.

Mahler, M., Pine, F., & Bergman, A., *The Psychological Birth of the Human Infant: Symbiosis and Individuation*, Basic Books, New York, 1975.

Makay, H., *Swim with the Sharks Without Being Eaten*, William Morrow, New York, 1988.

Makay, H., *Beware the Naked Man Who Offers You His Shirt*, William Morrow, New York, 1990.

McCormack, M., *What They Don't Teach You at Harvard Business School: Notes from a Street Smart Executive*, Bantam Books, New York, 1984.

Miller, A., *The Drama of the Gifted Child*, Basic Books, New York, 1981.

Miller, A., *For Your Own Good: Hidden Cruelty in Child Rearing and the Roots of Violence*, Farrar, Straus, & Giroux, New York, 1983.

Miller, A., *Thou Shalt Not Be Aware: Society's Betrayal of the Child*, Basic Books, New York, 1984.

Napier, A., & Wittiker, C., *The Family Crucible*, Harper & Row, New York, 1978.

Neisser, V., *Cognition and Reality*, W.H. Freeman, San Francisco, CA, 1976.

O'Keefe, B., *Shooting Ourselves in the Foot*, Houghton Mifflin, Boston, MA, 1985.

Peacock, W., *Corporate Combat: Military Strategies That Win Business Wars*, Berkeley, New York, 1984.

Pearson, C., *Awakening the Heroes Within*, HarperCollins, New York, 1981.

Pearson, C., *The Hero Within*, HarperCollins, New York, 1989.

Perles, F., *Gestalt Therapy Verbatim*, Bantam Books, New York, 1969.

Pinchot III, G., *Intrapreneuring*, Harper & Row, New York, 1985.

Porter, C., Lawler, E., & Packman, J., *Behavior in Organizations*, McGraw-Hill, New York, 1975.

Reed, S., *Toxic Executive*, HarperCollins, New York, 1993.

Reeves, T., *A Question of Character*, Random House, New York, 1991.

Ries, A., & Trout, J., *Positioning: The Battle for Your Mind*, McGraw-Hill, New York, 1981.

Ries, A., & Trout, J., *Marketing Warfare*, McGraw-Hill, New York, 1986.

Sager, C., *Marriage Contracts and Couple Therapy: Hidden Forces in Intimate Relationships*, Brunner/Mazel, New York, 1976.

Satir, V., *Conjoint Family Therapy*, Science and Behavior Books, Inc., New York, 1967.

Schaef, A. W., *Beyond Therapy, Beyond Science*, HarperCollins, New York, 1992.

Schaef, A. W., & Fassel, D., *The Addictive Organization*, Harper-Collins, New York, 1988.

Skynner, R., *Systems of Family and Martial Psychotherapy*, Brunner/Mazel, New York, 1976.

Stein, A., *Comprehensive Family Therapy: In the Psychotherapy Handbook*, New American Library, New York, 1980.

Trilling, L., & Marcus, S., (Eds.), *The Life and Work of Sigmund Freud*, Basic Books, New York, 1961.

Tzu, S., *The Art of War*, Shambhala Publications, Boston, MA, 1988.

Wright, J. P., *On a Clear Day You Can See General Motors*, Avon Books, New York, 1979.

INDEX